STO

reducing after forty

G. S. SERINO M.D.

A VERTEX BOOK
Princeton   New York   Philadelphia   London

1598754

To my wife Kathleen

Contents

PART TWO
THE EIGHT REDUCING DIETS

APPENDIXES

Preface

There are many excellent books available on reducing—a subject which, for many reasons, holds interest for the majority of American adults. However, most of these works deal with the problem in a general way and for a universal readership. As far as I am aware, there is little information available on the reducing problem faced by those in middle age. This book is for them.

In dealing with overweight we cannot discuss or treat it by itself: it must be approached on an individual basis taking into consideration each person's health and other circumstances. And dieting cannot be successful unless the person dieting has an elementary knowledge of nutritional laws.

I hope that those who read this book will, with some professional help, be able to help themselves and others. Overweight is a problem which has a solution. There is no quick or miracle cure; but the best opinions of modern science, which I have embodied in these pages, should enable overweight middle-agers to cope with the problem intelligently and successfully.

G.S.S.

PART ONE

THE MANY APPROACHES TO DIETING

CHAPTER ONE

Forty and Beyond

Every advance in medical science lengthens our horizons of longevity. Most children born today have every chance of living well into their seventies. Within the next decade we can expect significant discoveries in the treatment of the most dreaded ailments, including cancer and heart disease. With each step forward we have to revise our attitudes toward the various stages of life.

Middle age is a handy, general term which covers the 40-to-65-year period of life. Only a few generations ago men and women regarded it as the last lap of life. This is longer the case and we can look at that period of living with brighter and more hopeful eyes. Yesterday the talents of research conquered the great diseases of childhood: smallpox, diphtheria, polio, scarlet fever. Today most branches of medicine are focused on middle life, and we know far more about it than ever before, although we have a lot to learn.

Talleyrand, the famous French diplomat, used to remind his friends that "everybody wants to live long, but nobody wants to be old." Aging is a baffling mystery: the gradual, almost imperceptible decline of the agility and powers of the body. This process—the struggle between the forces that destroy body tissues and those that build it up—is a lifelong process. We become more aware of it as we enter middle age and reassess our lives and ambitions.

For a woman, entering middle life is rather crucial. Her menopause is approaching. Her family has grown; some of her children are talking or thinking of marriage; she has more leisure and can give a little more time to herself. She cannot stave off the menopause, yet she doesn't fret about it as much as her mother did. American women generally take a pragmatic view of the inevitable and do something about it. They often become more beauty-conscious, devote more care to their personal appearance, and make the "watch-my-weight" resolution.

Man glides more smoothly into middle life. Usually he is seasoned and mature; his ambitions are more or less defined; he senses that he is fit for responsibility in his work. Of course he is becoming conscious that he is a little more settled in his tastes and ways. For a man early middle life has been called "the danger period." Some, anxious to prove that youthful vigor is very much with them, have an urge to play around and pay more attention to younger women. But for all there is a realization that it is time to be a little more anxious about health —and weight.

Sociologists have some gloomy things to tell us about early middle life. They point out that it marks an upswing in the divorce rate, an increased incidence of alcoholism. True. But these social and psychological problems, which erupt and surface in the early middle life, have roots that are years old. It is only natural that they occur at this period of readjustment and changing circumstances.

Yet most modern men and women take the advent of middle age in their stride. They enter it with high hopes seasoned by experience. And there is no doubt that they gradually become more aware of and interested in the ailments which so often mar this period of life: coronary heart trouble, peptic ulcers, diabetes. Researchers note that they are keenly sensitive to the fact that overweight is a definite health hazard and is somehow connected with some of the common ailments of middle life.

Mature men and women, in their forties and beyond, are weight conscious—for the sake of both health and appearance. In this book I deal with the problem of overweight, its causes and cures. As a doctor I offer advice based on the research of modern medicine and the experience of many years of observation. Overweight is a common problem. Those who face and solve it are happier and healthier during the great years of middle life.

CHAPTER TWO

Overweight: Heredity and Environment

Frequently doctors hear overweight patients remark: "It's a family problem, my father (or mother) was always on the heavy side." Of course from a medical viewpoint this rarely means very much: The balance of evidence indicates that heredity has very little to do with overweight problems.

We inherit physical characteristics (shape and size) but we cannot blame our forebears for the excess fat we carry around. There are exceptions but these are rare. In stating this position we must glance at some seemingly established facts, which seem to indicate otherwise. Surveys have shown that when one parent is very much overweight at least one of the offspring develops the same problem. This is true in 85 percent of cases investigated. When both parents are overweight the incidence jumps to 95 percent. However, we cannot leap to the conclusion that hereditary factors are the culprit and cause. Environment plays a far greater role.

Consider an actual case. Identical twins were born in New York to parents with overweight problems. Due to a respiratory debility, one was sent to Arizona to live with relatives. The twin who remained at home grew in wisdom and weight; his brother maintained normal weight, except when he returned home for a long stay— then he really put on pounds. I met the parents and both children: they were worried about the weight of the healthy twin. The other was normal—but they attributed this to his respiratory debility. On questioning both boys on what they liked to eat, I quickly discovered that the obese child had developed a taste for the fattening diet of his parents; the other had not.

I have come across middle-aged patients who feel that their weight problem was inevitable since their parents, or at least one of them, had had the same difficulty. However, when I question them, I almost always come to the same conclusion: genes have nothing to do with it; environment and menu are the root of the problem. (Of course we are not discussing "glandular obesity," which is a rare occurrence and has little to do with overeating or eating the wrong foods. In a minority of cases glandular obesity may have a hereditary connection.)

Race, religion, and culture have a bearing on the problem of overweight. For instance: the American Irish are very fond of the potato (have you ever dined with one who doesn't order an Idaho and all the trimmings with his steak?). But when they become weight-conscious, it becomes a little difficult to ask them to hit a potatoless diet. I take this as an example of national heritage; each nationality has its own.

It has been pointed out that some peoples exhibit a greater tendency to obesity than others. For instance: the Dutch are proverbially as stout as the Americans are thin. Two main reasons explain this: the national Dutch dishes—Dutch coffee table, Dutch pea soup, rijsttafel—are high in calories; and secondly, the Dutch are not a weight-conscious people. In America fighting weight is on every woman's mind, and men are becoming deeply involved in the weight battle also. But in Holland the tradition (now changing) rests on the fact that a fat person is a monument to a good home and good feeding. There are some sociological factors involved here: the longer a family has American roots, the less likely are its members to be overweight. In the usual ethnic ghetto obesity will be common; the next generation moves out and rises socially and the rate of obesity declines. An interesting New York survey showed that those at the top of the social sale had a 5 percent obesity incidence, the middle stratum 16 percent, and a poor ghetto area 30 percent. When both parents are fourth-generation Americans, they and their offspring are not likely to have overweight problems. One explanation would be the consciousness that obesity is not part of the American ideal; only the American who has moved away from national dishes—and poverty—can be truly selective.

Nevertheless it is strange that American children develop overweight problems more frequently than Europeans. This may be because American children have a greater opportunity to overeat. And their permissive parents give them almost everything they like to eat.

The incidence of obesity among women in a poor national-group area runs six times higher than in a well-to-do area. And among men the ratio is two-to-one. The reason is the different outlooks toward weight and the use of high-calorie foods. These American findings are also borne out by a 1963 German survey, which reflects the fact that immigrants (and there are millions in Germany now) are more inclined to live together in national groups, sticking to native dishes, while other more prosperous citizens are more weight-conscious and more discriminating in their eating habits. National traditions break down slowly: Italian-American women, retaining their fondness for family recipes, have twice the overweight rate of that of women of British ancestry.

The German-Americans are enthusiastic about fattening foods, and this even shows up in a socio-religious breakdown: Lutherans (most of German extraction) have an occurrence of obesity eight times higher than Episcopalians (most of British descent). Germans, with a traditional love of home food, stick to a fattening diet, while the British have less of a problem, for Britain is a country with generally much simpler home foods.

The orthodox Jewish Community which follows the dietary laws has little problem with overweight. Religion is an influencing factor, just as is the cultural and ethnic background which I have described above.

So, when advising a middle-aged overweight person, it is essential to take several environmental factors into consideration. A solution to the problem is not difficult: a balanced and palatable diet (which takes the personal tastes and environmental possibilities into consideration) and exercise (suited to the temperament of the person) can work wonders. A stringent and penitential program won't work; we must strive for the ideal in weight control, and arrange for the possible. This is why the program I outline will, or should, be of little burden to those who follow it.

CHAPTER THREE

Caloric Requirements

The number of calories required to maintain life and provide energy for work varies from person to person. The minimum requirement to maintain life is called *basal metabolism*. This is reckoned when the person is at rest and the activities of the body are at slow gear. For men the average basal metabolism is 1700 calories; for women it is 1300. Once this is established, it is possible to proceed and reckon the *total metabolism:* the calorie requirements for normal work and activities. There is no one formula for deciding the energy needs of any individual. A number of factors must be considered.

WORK

Occupations can, for the sake of working clarity, be divided into four categories.

1. Sedentary work—receptionist
2. Moderate work—housewife

3. Heavy work—house painter
4. Very heavy work—dock worker

All activity consumes energy—the more restful the posture the less energy required. A glance at the average calorie output in various chores clarifies this point. A receptionist in a company office expends only 14 to 40 calories per hour; a student in a relaxed thinking mood uses 7 to 8 "work" calories per hour; the woman vacuuming floors releases about 216 calories; a lumberjack uses up 480 calories in his normal hour's work.

The following comparison (Table 1) shows the daily energy consumption in two common occupations.

Table 1. Daily Calorie Consumption, Sedentary/Active

Activity	Clerk	Laborer
Metabolism of sleeping	520	520
Basal metabolism	1150	1150
Nonwork allowance	400	400
Work consumption	300	3040
	2370	5110

If we add another 10 percent for dynamic and functional activities such as digestion, the clerk requires 2370 plus 240 calories per day; the laborer 5110 plus 510 for his normal daily living.

Research shows that a man in a sedentary occupation burns up 225 calories per day (225 for a woman also in the same type of work); in a moderate type of work a man burns up 750 calories (a woman 500); in heavy work a man consumes 1500 (a woman 1000). And in very heavy work a man uses 2500 calories (women in the United States, though, are rarely engaged in these activities). From this it is obvious that a woman uses up less work-calories than a man. Consequently her weight problem is, as statistics show, more prevalent than that of a man. In middle life we find ten women with weight problems for every man with the same.

EATING HABITS

A person's eating habits reflect both his background and his personal taste. A person who is overweight requires more calories on account of his condition. His basal and total metabolism counts are higher. His increased basal requirements are 600 calories per day more than the average man. Many fat men deny that they are big eaters. This is, on the whole, a self-deception. They eat average meals, but nibble between them. They may skip breakfast, eat a light lunch, and avoid nibbling between meals, but they will eat a huge dinner. Many such people think they are dieting because they have only one decent meal a day, forgetting the vital fact that it is not the number of meals that matters, but the total daily calorie intake.

Another practice of the overweight middle-agers is to diet during working days and to make up for the austerity by gorging over the weekend. But there are people whose failing is their culinary taste: they may not eat too much, but they just like the calorie-laden foods. This is the case with about 20 percent of overweight men and women.

The psychological state of the person often leads to careless dieting. A woman or man who is living in tension either overeats or seeks relief in alcohol. Many married couples who experienced a marital crisis for a few months found that they both had developed weight problems, even though they didn't notice that they were eating too much, overdrinking or exercising too little during the crisis. A worried person rarely is in the mood to count calories.

It is obvious from the above that in the overweight cases more calories are taken in than are burned up.

There is one curious fact: mental activity has no effect whatever on weight problems. The mental activity of a laborer and a scholar account for the same calorie usage. So in mapping out a calorie program, mental activity is not a factor.

With increasing years the calorie requirements reduce gradually. The following chart (Table 2) shows the calories required at various age stages. The middle-ager, after reducing, must never exceed the calorie count outlined.

Table 2. Daily Calorie Needs According to Desirable
Body Weight and Age (Average Physical Activity)

DESIRABLE WEIGHT	CALORIE ALLOWANCE		
Pounds	25 Years	45 Years	65 Years
MEN			
110	2300	2050	1750
121	2450	2200	1850
132	2600	2350	1950
143	2750	2500	2100
154	2900	2600	2200
165	3050	2750	2300
176	3200	2900	2450
187	3350	3050	2550
WOMEN			
88	1600	1450	1200
99	1750	1600	1300
110	1900	1700	1450
121	2000	1800	1550
128	2100	1900	1600
132	2150	1950	1650
143	2300	2050	1750
154	2400	2200	1850

Source: Food and Nutrition Board, National Research Council.

CHAPTER FOUR

Normal Weight, Normal Diet

The words "normal" and "abnormal" perplex people, and no wonder. They are relative words we use loosely or wrongly. There has been much research and debate on what is the normal or desirable weight for middle-aged men and women. Opinions differ slightly, and the following chart, graded according to body frame, gives a general average on this question. The chart allows about eight pounds for men's clothing and four pounds for women's.

I am concerned here with overweight men and women in the 40-to-65 age group, and what is normal for them would be totally abnormal for a more active teenager.

Here are some criteria for any basic diet for anyone willing to reduce. They apply to diets for all age groups but particularly for the 40-to-65 group.

The diet must:

1. supply all the essential nutrients necessary for normal living

Table 3. Normal Weight—Men

HEIGHT (WITH SHOES ON)		WEIGHT IN POUNDS (AS ORDINARILY DRESSED, INCLUDING SHOES AND SUIT)		
Feet	Inches	Small frame	Medium frame	Large frame
5	2	112–120	118–129	126–141
5	3	115–123	121–133	129–144
5	4	118–126	124–136	132–148
5	5	121–129	127–139	135–152
5	6	124–133	130–143	138–156
5	7	128–137	134–147	142–161
5	8	132–141	138–152	147–166
5	9	136–145	142–156	151–170
5	10	140–150	146–160	155–174
5	11	144–154	150–165	159–179
6	0	148–158	154–170	164–184
6	1	152–162	158–175	168–189
6	2	156–167	162–180	173–194
6	3	160–171	167–185	178–199
6	4	164–175	172–190	182–204

2. be balanced and easily digestible
3. be easily available at reasonable cost
4. conform to the eating habits of the individual and give a feeling of satiety and pleasure
5. offer a balance between bulk food and liquid

Much research has gone into a normal diet. The UN World Health Organization and the Food and Nutrition Board of the National Research Council have published general guidelines, but these are no more than general. The dieting individual must consult his doctor for specific and safe advice. Climate, weight, physical

Normal Weight—Women

		Small frame	Medium frame	Large frame
HEIGHT (WITH SHOES ON)		**WEIGHT IN POUNDS (AS ORDINARILY DRESSED, INCLUDING SHOES AND DRESS)**		
Feet	Inches			
4	10	92–98	96–107	104–119
4	11	94–101	98–110	106–122
5	0	96–104	101–113	109–125
5	1	99–107	104–116	112–128
5	2	102–110	107–119	115–131
5	3	105–113	110–122	118–134
5	4	108–116	113–126	121–138
5	5	111–119	116–130	125–142
5	6	114–123	120–135	129–146
5	7	118–127	124–139	133–150
5	8	122–131	128–143	137–154
5	9	126–135	132–147	141–158
5	10	130–140	136–151	145–163
5	11	134–144	140–155	149–168
6	0	138–148	144–159	153–173

make-up, and daily activity have a bearing on a balanced diet.

But the middle-aged individual needs less calories than a younger person. A person in the 40-to-65 age group can do with 8 to 10 percent less calories than those in their twenties or early thirties.

The difference in basic needs, and the necessity of expert medical advice can be gauged from the following. The normal caloric requirements in America varies from 2100 to 2900; in Holland, 2400 to 3000; in Australia, 2300 to 2700; in Japan, 2400 to 3000; in India 2300 to 2800; in Norway, 2500 to 3400. These requirements are tabulated for the person engaged in moderate work. Of course, the figure rises once the individual engages in heavy work or taxing exercise.

In speaking of a normal reducing diet the total health of the individual must be of primary concern. A diet for a person with diabetic tendencies or trouble should differ from that prescribed for a heart patient or for a person with no health problem except overweight. So there is no such thing as a perfect reducing diet: it must vary from person to person. Every balanced diet should have carbohydrates, fats, proteins, vitamins, and minerals, and we shall now discuss each of these separately.

CHAPTER FIVE

The Basic Ingredients of any Diet

The perfect diet doesn't exist. Neither is there a beneficial diet that suits all people. But throughout history
Western man has sought to find the easy, sure-to-work
diet that would take care of unwanted weight. Today we
have a dieting fad on a national scale; and recently, a
doctor remarked that Americans are the "world champion
calorie counters." But, even though calories count, the
approach is defective, for many reasons. And to add to
the weight dilemma, most popular diets are defective.
Only recently, Dr. Fred L. Allman, Jr., who is a recog-
nized expert on nutritional problems, surveyed and tor-
pedoed most of the diets on which athletes are supposed
to thrive.

The modern fad diets don't change much from age
to age, despite the advances of nutritional medicine. Take
a random example: a mortician in London named John
Banting (who is remembered in the footnotes in history
because he made the casket for the Duke of Wellington)

published a booklet in 1864 in which he presented his "miracle" high fat–high protein diet. He swore that while on this diet he lost 46 pounds in one year, even though he never denied himself a few glasses of whisky each day. His diet, with variations, is still recommended by many who never heard of him. So is Dr. von Noorden's famous high protein–moderate carbohydrate diet, promulgated a little later. Almost every year of every decade for the last century has brought its new dieting program, but essentially they repeat one another. After he had viewed in perplexity all the reducing diets of his day, it is no wonder that Sir William Osler, regarded by many as the father of modern medicine, advised that the only sure way of reducing was simply to cut down on eating.

On analysis, the main problem is not to shed unwanted weight quickly; it is better to shed it permanently. Time and the experience of generations has proved that fad diets and stringent formulas don't work. The balanced, tolerable diet is the only kind that will succeed. But we are not talking just about dieting to counter overweight, but rather a new attitude, one that entails a coordinated approach: balanced living, with a nourishing diet, proper rest, and enjoyable exercise.

Before going further it is essential to have a grasp of the basic terms and the main ingredients of foods.

CARBOHYDRATES

Carbohydrates is a cover-all term. The word is commonly applied to sugars and starches. When we describe a food high or low in carbohydrates, we simply mean that it is high or low in the amount of sugar or starch it contains. In discussing any diet, we divide carbohydrates into categories: *natural* (consumed in the natural state, such as potatoes, fruit, whole wheat bread), and *refined* (processed food, such as candy, sugar, ice cream). For the dieter and for a balanced diet, it is wise to cut refined carbohydrates to the minimum. This is a simple workable principle. But it would be a health hazard to cut out carbohydrates indiscriminately. We need them as the prime, quick source of heat and energy.

FATS

Fat can be described as a compound containing glycerine (a thick, sweet, colorless liquid) and a variety of fatty acids. When speaking of fats, dietitians usually classify them as *saturated* and *unsaturated* fats, each of which contains certain fatty acids. For example, butyric acid (found in butter and other dairy products), and palmitic and stearic acids (found in animal fats and certain vegetable oils) are associated with saturated fats. Oleic, linoleic, and linolenic acids (found in oils made from corn, soybeans, peanuts, cotton seeds, sunflower seeds, etc.) are associated with unsaturated fats. Saturated fats raise the cholesterol blood level (this is one reason why they should be cut to the minimum in a diet for middle-agers), but unsaturated fats have the opposite effect. Fat, as it burns itself up in the body, yields heat and energy, but as it is a poor conductor of heat, it protects the body

from rapid cooling. Its other beneficial, salutary diet traits
are: it can be stored and it is essential to the development
and repair of the body cells; it slows down digestion and,
in doing so, delays and retards hunger pangs.

PROTEINS

Proteins, the prime tissue and cell builders of the
body, are absolutely essential to life. They are classified
as high or low, depending on the type of amino acids they
contain. Each acid plays a specific role in the functioning
of the body. For middle-agers, a more-than-minimum
intake of protein is highly recommended. The Food and
Drug Administration advises that a man of 150 pounds
should have a daily protein intake of at least 70 grams;
the diet of a 127-pound woman should contain at least 58
grams. When selecting the protein element of your diet,
it is essential that you choose foods you like; and remember that in meats the wastage of protein (which should always be a part of any diet) is far higher than in vegetables.

VITAMINS AND MINERALS

The balanced diet provides all the vitamins you
require, and the same is true for your mineral—(iron
and calcium)—requirements. Middle-agers, especially
women, have to be careful during and after the meno-

pause. Anemia, which is an iron deficiency, can surreptitiously occur. To counteract it make sure that you have a diet with a more-than-sufficient iron content.

As we grow older through middle age, our bones grow more brittle. So it is wise to have a counteracting and ample supply of calcium in our meals.

CHAPTER SIX

Exercise

Most Europeans have convinced themselves, and many of us, that America is a go-go nation—activist, exercise-mad, talkative, and restless. They presume that leisure is not part of our way of life, and most of us believe the same thing. But stop and consider things as they really are: in our personal lives we are perhaps the least activist nation on earth. We exercise too little—for, as a predominantly urban and suburban people, we have neither the time nor the opportunity for enjoyable exercise. I use the word "enjoyable" because unless exercise sparks our interest and gives us pleasure, it is no more than a chore.

Talking to middle-agers over the years, I have reached a decision that many of them, especially if they are overweight, have a mild exercise complex. "Doctor, should I exercise?" The question is so common that it tends to become irrelevant and one is driven to answer "When—and how?" Only the patient can answer this. Take a middle-aged man who drives to work each day, walks to the nearest cafe for lunch, drives home, has a relaxing pre-dinner drink, and spends the evening watching TV or reading business or news magazines and tell him to get out and walk for an hour or play golf. It is a futile proposal if he has no interest whatsover in either. I prefer to toss the problem back: "If you had the time, what exercise would you enjoy most?" Once a person can answer this question, then a doctor can help. It is almost instinctive for patients to feel that they should have some regular exercise schedule. Once they delineate their preference, a doctor can be of great help. Exercise is helpful for any middle-aged person, and it is essential in the reducing program of anyone with an overweight problem; but it must be enjoyable and regular.

One of the suspicions that haunts a doctor when dealing with overweight patients is the possibility of heart trouble. An amount of research has gone into this question—and the findings converge on one conclusion: planned and suitable exercise can and does alleviate the incidence and help the cure of heart ailments. One of the greatest heart specialists of this century, Dr. Paul Dudley White of Boston, has, time and again, appealed to Americans to exercise. Dr. Eldrid Smith has proved that never again can a heart patient afford to sit still, lie down, or worry; he has to get up and exercise if he wants to improve.

I had an overweight heart patient, who loved dogs and lived in an apartment. Each time she came to me, I found that she inevitably turned to her dream of owning a big dog. She hated exercise. In the end I told her to get an Irish setter, informing her that this type of dog had to be "walked" for three or four miles each day or else it would become lethargic. She got the dog, walked him for hours each day, and enjoyed it—and her weight and heart condition improved. The dog insured that she would exercise each day, and that dog was her best friend.

One of the important things for people over 40 is to develop new interests. To avoid getting into a rut, they should develop a new hobby or expand their work interests, but, more importantly, they should try to discover a form of *active* interest which appeals to them.

Exercise offers many benefits to the middle-ager, whether his weight is normal or not. Regular exercise restores or maintains normal muscle tone. It improves circulation and benefits the health of the heart. It increases the rate of inhalation and this aids the lungs. Exercise increases the rate of metabolism, by increasing the oxidation of food consumed. It helps to relieve tension, to shed excessive weight, and it aids digestion.

Turning to the weight problem, it is obvious that the benefits of exercise are especially appropriate here. As mentioned previously, the choice of exercise should suit the temperament, age, and physical health of an individual. For instance: if a person is inclined to worry he would not benefit much by lone walking, which would only become a time to worry more. Such a person would benefit most by some group or social activity, which would help him to forget his cares.

The following two charts will give the reader a good idea of the worth of various types of exercise in a reducing program.

With some forethought and planning, a person could bank on losing about a pound each week with any of these exercises.

	Calorie output per week
Push-ups, ½ hour weekly	770
Golf, 18 holes, 3 times weekly	1800
Dancing, 1 hour daily	1190
Walking, ½ hour daily	770
Gardening, 5 hours weekly	1500
Swimming, 3 hours weekly	1500
Cycling, 4 hours weekly	1600
Walking at a brisk pace, 3 hours weekly	1200
Tennis, 6 hours weekly	1250
Volleyball, 6 hours weekly	1500
Bowling, 5 hours weekly	800

To look at the benefits of exercise from another angle, the following facts are helpful:

	Calorie output per hour
Walking, moderately	220
Walking, briskly	400
Running	800
Cycling	400
Swimming	500
Light exercise	85
Active exercise	205
Gardening	300

There are some people who reduce by dieting and ignore exercise. But a regimen of enjoyable exercise and a good balanced diet is far more beneficial and will produce better results all around.

CHAPTER SEVEN

Water and Weight

Water plays a major role in the normal functioning of the body. As a matter of fact, no living organism could exist without it. Fortunately the world has its water abundance: some 70 percent of the earth's surface is covered by water—and, by coincidence, water accounts for 70 percent of the weight of the human body.

For three distinct reasons, I should like to say a short word about water and reducing. First, many people erroneously cut down on water intake during a diet. Second, many overweight men and women develop a "water problem." Third, in the first round of a reducing regimen middle-agers often become elated or depressed by a sudden decrease or increase in weight: this is due to a temporary imbalance in what we call man's water equilibrium.

Before discussing water and weight, let's consider the main function of water in the human system.

We are basically water-men: our blood is 90 percent water and this "conveyer" and "solvent" performs so many functions that we shall enumerate only a few: water runs the respiratory system, transporting oxygen from the air to the lungs and from there to the body cells and tissues; then it carries the waste product carbon dioxide from the tissues to the lungs from which the gas is exhaled. It conveys all the nutrition needed by the tissues. Water, because of its nature, is the regulator of body temperature.

The body is a complex of delicate systems. Any extraordinary encounter or occurrence upsets its working. A fat person can go along with a perfect water balance for years. Then he decides to reduce and the balance is immediately upset. In the first days of his reducing he can gain weight! What has happened? He has lost his water balance and is retaining too much water. Or he may drop as much as ten pounds in the first days of his regimen. He hasn't shed fat—just water. His water balance has gone out of gear temporarily.

Many patients decide to restrict their intake of water during their reducing program. This is a mistake. Weight and water are not connected. And some reducers ask their doctors to prescribe diuretics (water pills) to regulate their urinary functions. This is hardly necessary; the water balance usually rights itself within two weeks.

On an average, our daily intake of water in liquid or in food (the average steak is 70 percent water) is six to eight glasses or about one and a half quarts; our output (through urination, sweating, and so on) is about the same. Thus we have a water equilibrium: an approximate balance between intake and output. Water intake adds to your weight, accidentally. It does not have anything to do with your weight problem: water has no calories and does not mix with fat. So, it is an extraneous factor.

Those who cut down on their water consumption while dieting or reducing miss a vital point. The body has a tendency to maintain a water balance. If you cut down your consumption, automatically you feel thirsty, among other things, and the activity of your kidneys slows down.

So take little or no notice of the weight variations in the first week of your reducing program. Your water balance may be out of tune: wait for two weeks before evaluating your success. By then your water balance will have adjusted itself.

Weight watchers in middle age should not be afraid to go near water; it has nothing to do with the weight problem.

CHAPTER EIGHT

To Nibble or Gorge

The longer one lives the more one wonders at the motivation of some human actions. Every day doctors confront patients whom they are trying to help but who won't put all the facts on the table. This type of patient feels he must present himself in the best light to the doctor. One of the reasons that medical opinions are still inconclusive on the relationship between eating patterns and overweight is that research based on information supplied by patients has led to conflicting conclusions. From long experience, I think that some patients, especially women, hesitate to give a total accounting of their food intake. They will tell you what they eat at the table, but will avoid mentioning the snacks and the sampling of food which they enjoyed. This raises the question which many middle-aged people with weight problems ask: "Should I eat regular meals and avoid all other snacks or food sampling, or should I avoid big meals and resort to frequent snacking or nibbling?"

Many doctors advise patients to nibble and avoid big meals. Others take an opposite course. Either course raises questions. Since the person with a weight problem eats too much of everything or eats too much of fattening foods, I believe that the patient's eating pattern, whether he nibbles constantly or gorges infrequently, makes little difference. What matters is the kind of food and the quantity consumed. This is the best answer I can give—with some minor qualifications.

WOMEN

As stated before, many more women in their middle years have weight problems than men. They tend to opt for carbohydrate-heavy food and their unbalanced diet is often low in protein. The female body has by nature proportionately more fat than the male, but this does not account for the higher ratio of overweight women among people between the ages of 40 and 65. Women are more addicted to nibbling than men. A woman, working in the kitchen or preparing meals, almost unconsciously is inclined to taste the food. During the day she is more tempted to snack and nibble and it is unusual for a woman to prefer a huge meal or meals at fixed times. But the overweight woman doesn't usually keep track of her between-meal eating. To prove this point, a research team put six obese women under supervision. In clinical surroundings, they could order what they liked and as much as they wanted for regular meals. Nibbling, however, was not permitted. Over a ten-week period they each lost an average of 20 pounds. Kitchen food-tasting and nibbling made the difference.

MEN

The average obese or overweight man tells his doctor he can abstain from eating and drinking between meals. Some forego breakfast, eat a normal lunch but gorge at the dinner table. Others stick to normal-sized meals but can't resist raiding the icebox before retiring at night. Still others can control eating during the work week but go on an "eating binge" during the weekend. It is a known fact that overweight men tend to cut down on physical exercise and to drink a little more of alcoholic drinks. In a supervised study of eight obese men over a four-day period, each was asked to drink and eat as he would at home, and each lost an average of eight pounds. Another test showed that it made little or no difference if a man ate six small meals or one large one—if the calorie content of the six meals was the same as the one.

The only reasonable conclusion based on the above studies, and many others, is that the eating habits of an overweight person don't matter. The nibbler who nibbles too much or the one-mealer who gorges once daily are both in the same boat: their calorie intake is too much. Calories count, whether they are supplied at one meal or many over a 24-hour period.

CHAPTER NINE

Overweight and Alcoholic Beverages

By the age of 40, most men and women have begun to live their days in a regular and semi-fixed pattern. They tend to approach life sensibly, and usually the clock has a bigger part to play in their daily routine than when they were younger. They rise and retire at regular hours; they get to work and leave at fixed times. And most worry a little more about health and wealth. It is the beginning of the age of prudence, and they feel that it is a time to watch the waistline and to evaluate some taken-for-granted habits. Once the question of weight begins to worry them, it is only a short step to the question: "how do my drinking habits affect my weight?"

When discussing drinking I am, of course, discussing moderate alcoholic consumption. True alcoholism cannot be taken up in a book discussing the weight problem; it is a far more serious problem than obesity for any man or woman. And as doctors know from long experience, it is extremely difficult to treat a chronic drinker for any ailment: the bottle runs the show and advice is rarely followed. Therefore, the question here is moderate drinking only, or rather the relationship between your drinking and its possible effect on your weight problem.

All alcoholic beverages are classified as foods. Besides furnishing calories or energy, they also provide a varying percentage of carbohydrates, vitamins, and minerals, depending on the drink. In discussing weight these factors must be reckoned with. But primarily we must remember that alcoholic drinks can provide 100 or more calories per ounce of alcohol consumed.

While alcoholic drinks are not essential foods, nevertheless they add a welcome sparkle to eating, and they can create a relaxed mood in the tense and weary man or woman. Their tranquilizing, soothing effects help to make life more pleasant and our daily problems less pressing. For that reason I hesitate to ask any moderate drinker to forego the pleasure of a few daily drinks. If the relaxing effects are beneficial enough to the person worried about his weight, then compensating calorie-cutting can take place in other areas. However there are a few ground rules which should be noted and followed when a person decides not to forego the brew while dieting.

A generation ago drinking a dry sherry or other aperitif, such as the vermouths, Dubonnet, or Campari, was the accepted custom. Such light drinks were supposed to whet the appetite. They do, but not as much as a martini or a whiskey straight or sour—or for that matter any drink that is 80 proof (40 percent alcohol) or more. A cocktail or two taken before dinner is actually a two-edged sword: if drunk within 20 minutes before the meal is served it increases the desire for food. If consumed more than 20 minutes before the meal it seems to depress the appetite. At dinner parties hostesses have observed that if drink is liberally served for an hour or so before dinner, there are few calls for second helpings.

While drink can have a stimulating effect, as described above, its tranquilizing effect can aid obese patients who have an emotional problem which drives them to seek solace by overeating. Dr. Giorgio Lolli, of New York City, and his associates made studies with obese patients who had failed to shed weight by normal means. By giving them one and a half or two ounces of wine 30 to 60 minutes before dinner and before bedtime Lolli succeeded in getting the patients to cut down on food. Others have also found that a little wine with dinner helps to alleviate fatigue and make a diet meal more enjoyable. And if we don't enjoy our meals, then the burden of life and work becomes a little heavier, for meals have more than a nutritional function.

For those who must count their calories and reduce, it would seem that if they must make a choice between an extra potato or a drink, they might safely opt for the drink. It is a consoling fact for them—and we are mainly concerned with those in middle age—that those who drink moderately usually outlive the chronic drinker and the teetotaller!

Apart from the weight problem, many middle age patients worry about what their drinking might do to their liver. In fact, it has very little effect. Moderate drinking increases the liver fat, but this is such a minor increase that it can be ignored.

So as a general rule, the doctor will not ask the overweight patient to forego his relaxing drink. If the patient drinks daily, the doctor will consider this when he's advising for a suitable diet. If the patient is a very casual and spasmodic drinker—the two-drinks-a-party man—the doctor will just ignore it.

Some authorities believe it essential to keep the "penance" aspect of the therapy as light as possible. For that reason they recommend a little wine rather than the more potent drinks with their high calorie count. Table wines have an average of 24.4 calories per ounce, and cocktail (or fortified) wines have 45.4 calories per ounce. It is easy for a doctor to prescribe a diet, but it is sometimes supremely difficult for a patient to follow it. For that reason, the suggestion of a little wine with the main meal appears a sensible one—and middle-aged people appreciate anything that smacks of common sense.

Reaching a general conclusion, we can state that moderate drinking may help more than hurt the patient, but it must be taken into consideration when making the daily calorie count. For that reason I have listed the calorie (and carbohydrate) content of the most popular drinks in the diet section contained in Part II of this book.

CHAPTER TEN

Should I Smoke?

Throughout the centuries peoples of all cultures have resorted to drugs for many and varied reasons: to assuage the agony of living; to provide religious experience; or just to get a "psychic lift" out of the humdrum course of everyday life. Each society has its special preference. The Indians favor hemp and its by-products. The Moslems opt for hashish. Orientals prefer opium and its alkaloids. Western society, as a whole, has turned to alcohol and tobacco. Tobacco is far less expensive, and it is commonly assumed that it is the less harmful of the two. But nicotine is a drug, and tobacco without nicotine is no longer tobacco—it gives as much pleasure as smoking old paper.

Americans have a reputation for being faddish about their health. Yet, there are over 70 million cigarette smokers in the country. And everytime they pick up a pack they read: "Warning: The Surgeon General Has Determined That Cigarette Smoking Is Dangerous To Your Health." This doesn't deter them (are they dubious of the claims and counterclaims of medical reformers?). At the present time a connection between lung cancer and cigarette smoking has been pretty well established; however,

the exact details of the connection are not yet fully clari-
fied. There is also considerable evidence that smoking
contributes to heart trouble and other ailments. But the
evidence is inconclusive as yet.

Why do people smoke? There is no easy answer.
Most get a physical and psychological pleasure out of it.
Some smoke to relieve tension. Others smoke simply because they enjoy it and their need of pleasure outweighs
the fear of possibly injuring their health.

Many health zealots believe that it would be a boon
to the nation if all cigarette smoking were banned. This
is a radical view, and an unwise one. Apart from the
question of freedom, studies have shown that some people
develop emotional troubles once they deprive themselves
of the weed; on resuming smoking their emotions balance
up again. For them, and for all who need the relief of a
smoke, moderation may be more sensible than abstention.
In dealing with anxious humanity doctors can sometimes
learn a little from the politician. To quote former Presi-
dent Lyndon B. Johnson: "We strive for the ideal and fix
for the possible."

Research on the link between smoking and weight is
just beginning. I have studied the results of most, if not
all, of the major experiments. The best that can be said
for them is that they establish very little, and often reach
contradictory conclusions. For instance, a study at Johns
Hopkins University indicated that those who were 30 to
40 percent overweight were mostly regular smokers,
while underweight people were not. It stated that
smokers were, as a group, more heavily built than nonsmokers. However, another study, by Albert Damon of
Harvard University, indicated that lean individuals

smoked more than fat ones. In spite of the contradictions, such research confirms much that most people suspect, even though they may not have given much thought to it.

SOME ESTABLISHED DATA ON SMOKING

At the beginning of middle age a smoking decline sets in. From the teen years to the age of 25 there is a steady and gradual increase in regular smoking: in America 60 percent of all men and 36 percent of all women have become semi-regular smokers. The percentage incidence continues to rise until the 40-year mark—and then a decline sets in. At the age of 60 only about 20 percent of American males and 4 percent of the women are smoking. Why? We don't know—but I believe that a major factor is fear; fear that smoking is injurious to their health, which they are now taking greater care of, drives many to quit smoking.

Yet when dealing with patients in the middle-age group who have weight worries, doctors are constantly asked: "Doctor should I smoke?"

With certain reservations I do not believe that smoking has a connection with anyone's weight problem. But we all know that people who are habitual smokers and decide to kick the habit put on weight rather quickly, often as much as 15 pounds in a six-week period. Once they give up smoking they can quell their desire for nicotine but they eat more. Cigarette smoking does have some tranquilizing effect, and when this is removed there is a psychological and physical urge to find a substitute. Most find it at the table or in the bar, or both. Once the nicotine habit is shaken, the appetite reverts to normal, and much of this excess weight, is shed, but not all of it.

A study done in 1957 at the Fels Foundation showed that those who gave up smoking gained an average of eight pounds over a two-year period, while nonsmokers of the same age and general physique gained only a pound. This shows clearly that when a person decides to go "smoke-less" he tends to seek compensation at the table.

It has also been observed that smoking immediately before meals tends to dull the appetite and the "taste buds." This is true over a short period, but usually as a long-distance practice it doesn't work. Yet if a person is very high-strung and living in constant tension, smoking a cigarette or two just before regular meals does help to curb the appetite.

However, those who at middle age quit smoking or those who never developed the habit should not turn to smoking to solve their weight problems—because it won't. Those overweight who smoke during their middle years are well advised to limit their habit: a smoke or two before the main meals, one cigarette after each meal, and an odd smoke in mid-morning and afternoon as a compensation for skipping the traditional snacks.

The most active smokers in middle age are those who work at "tension" jobs and those who do very little work at all. Their smoking has little or no bearing on their weight problems.

The weight problems that tend to come with middle life cannot be solved by smoking. The experience of men and the findings of researchers seem to verify the conclusion that smoking plays no role in weight therapy.

CHAPTER ELEVEN

Mental Attitudes and Overweight

The majority of overweight middle-agers can trace their problem to the table. Others, a very small minority, have a form of glandular obesity, not just simple overweight. But for the majority the big questions are: "Why do I eat too much?" "Why don't I diet and reduce?" "Why can't I stick to a diet?"

In many instances psychological factors are involved in middle-life weight problems. We live in a weight-conscious world. To a lesser degree all ages were concerned with it. From the age of Nero to the reign of Victoria, men and especially women have fretted about the disadvantages of excess weight. Today we worry and recently medical reports, widely disseminated, have added a touch of fear to our worry. We are convinced that the extra poundage is a health hazard. Modern man, attuned to having every aspect of his life and ailments set in a psychological perspective, may know he overeats but he eventually wants to know why.

Psychiatrists do not classify their patients by weight

—psychic ailments hit the light and the heavy. But they have noted that some middle-aged patients develop a weight problem as they seek a letup for their psychological problems. They have also noted that their obese patients with severe psychological problems have little success in coping with their overweight. With such patients, their psychic distress is a causative factor in their obesity. But to argue that all overweight problems are basically rooted in psychological factors is untenable. Very often in puberty overweight has a broad psychological basis: confronted with so many new and strange problems, sexual and otherwise, the young person has a tendency to eat or overeat in a search for solace. This is a very transitory factor for most.

Every doctor knows patients who realize that they should reduce but who say they can't tackle the problem. It would be more exact to say they don't want to. Basically their overweight is a protection wall. It does, as many of them claim, affect their social life. But they know that once they trim, their social relationship will change—and they dread the possible implications. This is true of a number of overweight bachelors and marriage-shy ladies. Their overweight is the means they use to evade some basic problems.

As a group, middle-agers are as psychologically normal as any other group. But they undergo some unique psychological strains at various stages: women in the menopause, men as they realize that they are not as agile as before, and in the sixties a sense of loneliness descends on many. At such times they feel that they deserve some compensation and that dieting is an undeserved chore. The temptation to overeat is a common temptation.

The first thing middle-agers have to realize and believe is that middle life is not old age, that good decades lie ahead. They must convince themselves that, for many good reasons, overweight is a great disadvantage. And they must feel that the effort to keep in shape or to shed excess weight is well worth the inconvenience involved. They should not be downcast because they have failed to reduce in their first attempt, for in the long run it is their deep determination that will make dieting possible, bearable, and successful.

Those in middle life who have solved their weight problem aver that they feel a tremendous sense of accomplishment and that this feeling in itself makes middle life an exciting time.

CHAPTER TWELVE

Sleep and Reduce

In the middle years sleep becomes a worry for many. In their early twenties and thirties people are inclined to exert themselves more, so that by bedtime they are readier for sleep. But the middle-aged man or woman, who is undergoing the physiological and psychological changes described earlier in this work, is inclined to be less active and more worried. Researchers tell us that 56 percent of American women and 49 percent of American men have some form of insomnia, and the majority of these are in the 40-to-65 age group. Some of these are people with a weight problem, so the question arises: "what effect has sleep on obesity?"

During sleep most bodily functions reduce to their basal levels—the minimum consumption of energy needed to keep the metabolic functions active. Blood pressure declines 10 to 30 points, reaching its lowest level at the fourth hour of sleep and continuing so until shortly before waking. Muscle tone reduces; urine volume decreases; respirations decline; stomach secretions increase slightly; heat regulating mechanisms are depressed; mouth (saliva) and eye (tear) secretion reduces.

From this we see that the physical changes in sleep are great; and it is obvious that the psychological "transformation" is also vast.

But there is one change that has a direct bearing on weight: during sleep the sweat glands are very active, and as much fluid is lost per hour as would be lost if the person performed exercise. This is the main physiological tie-up between sleep and reducing. Sleep helps; and the average overweight man or woman should try to get at least seven hours sleep every night.

But since many overweight problems have a direct or an indirect connection with psychological tension, it is most important that patients sleep soundly and well. Sleep enables us to handle tension and anxiety—and we know that many people try to ease their anxieties by overeating. Over the years I have noted that a good night's rest is one of the best preparations for a good day's dieting. The sleepless man or woman, wearied of tossing and turning, is tempted to get up and raid the refrigerator. So I offer the following ground rules to the overweight patient with a touch of insomnia.

1. Try not to worry about sleeplessness—better to rest awake in bed than walk and worry in pajamas around the living room—the kitchen is not too far away!
2. If worries keep you awake, talk them over (during the daytime) with your doctor or a sensible friend.
3. Resign yourself to some sleepless hours. Then you will probably doze off more quickly.
4. Don't eat before retiring.

5. Above all, prepare yourself for bedtime: avoid discussion of your work and worries; relax by fooling around with your hobby or by reading a light book or watching television.

So, relax, rest, and reduce!

CHAPTER THIRTEEN

Overweight, the Menopause, and the Andropause

The menopause is the most critical period in the life of every woman in middle age. The ending of menstruation is the final phase in a physiological process. This process develops over a long period and is marked by a complexity of symptoms. It begins with a gradual ovarian deficiency and terminates in the disappearance of periods.

This middle-age crisis usually (but not always) besets American women between the ages of 45 and 50. But since hereditary and many other factors play a role in the advent and intensity of the menopause, no specific or definite time can be pinpointed for its occurrence.

Menopausal troubles are many and rather well known. They are of gynecologic, metabolic-nutritional, and psychological nature. We are concerned here only with nutritional ones, and these are the least significant of menopausal disorders. Nutritional troubles during this change of life are well known. The tendency to put on weight is rather commonplace. There is a general loss of breast tissue and a shifting of weight to the hips. The decrease in muscular activity, as well as heredity and some unknown natural factors contribute to these changes.

The menopause and its accompanying troubles have been well covered in literature, medical and general. Look at the number of novels which deal with a menopausal theme, including Thomas Mann's famous *Black Swan*. But, in contrast, how little we know about the man's "change of life." As a matter of fact many doctors will only admit its existence with reservations.

I am inclined to say that very few men in their fifties or early sixties undergo the andropause. The symptoms most frequently connected with it are recurring bouts of tiredness; slight heats—of lesser intensity than the female "flashes"; change of skin texture; irritability; and above all a sharp decline in the sexual drive and a lessening of testicular secretion. But the andropause is really not a major factor in middle age, as the menopause is.

Doctors who treat various types of menopausal ailments confirm that overweight retards treatment and becomes a constant source of worry for the patient. When women reach the menopause they often undergo great psychic strain; many become despondent about their present troubles and the years ahead. A number console themselves at the table and put on unwanted weight, which is most difficult to shed later on. But they should remember that the change of life is not old age. They should be more careful of their diets and ask their doctors to prescribe diets high in protein, low in fat and sugar.

CHAPTER FOURTEEN

Overweight and Heart Disease

Salvador de Madariaga, the Spanish political historian, tells us that we can almost prove opposite propositions by the deft use of statistics. When one reads appeals for research funds for various diseases, a suspicion arises that in giving percentages ("10 percent of all Americans have. . . .", "12 percent have. . . .") fund-raising copy writers use their imaginations freely. Otherwise one would have to conclude that the health of the Republic is in desperate shape, which it obviously isn't.

We have no *complete* statistical record of deaths due to any particular disease. In dealing with obesity and heart disease we must rely on the partial figures of insurance companies. These are accurate, as far as they go. But they do not tell us how many people are daily *refused* insurance coverage because they are obese. An insurance company takes few risks.

Heart trouble, is, by far, the nation's greatest killer. Just look at the daily obituary notices or the weekly death notices of celebrities in the newsmagazines.

The cause of some but not all heart ailments is known. Arteriosclerosis—hardening of the arteries—is the most common; and it is directly or indirectly responsible for over half of all deaths registered in the United States. Its pathogenesis is unknown, but in many cases it can be arrested if discovered in its early stages. Doctors know that its potential danger is lessened by treating hypertension, adopting diet supervision, curtailing or prohibiting the patient's smoking and getting him to take regular exercise.

Many factors must be taken into consideration when prescribing for heart patients. Heredity is a major one. It is commonly accepted that heart trouble can run in families, although for different reasons. Tension is a factor and the man or woman who lives a tense life is more prone to a heart ailment than the more relaxed person. Some doctors hold that a high fat diet increases cholesterol in the blood and that this is a heart hazard—a theory that further research may well verify.

Racial or ethnic factors have nothing to do with heart trouble—this killer doesn't distinguish between race, color, or creed. But the incidence of heart disease is six times more common in men than in women. The trouble of many heart patients can often be traced to their inability to tolerate carbohydrates, and this is particularly true of heart patients who have had diabetes.

Those with high blood pressure develop coronary trouble three to five times more frequently than those with low or normal blood pressure. And statistically, heavy cigarette smokers are more frequently stricken with heart disease than nonsmokers. As to overweight and obesity, there are some difficulties, hypotheses, and proven facts, which we shall now discuss.

A common belief is that overweight is a passport to heart trouble. Western man has long taken this supposition for granted, and medical observations supported the idea. A century ago (1867) Dr. T. H. Tanner wrote, "Obesity does not conduce to longevity." Thirty years later Dr. D. Duckworth described it as "an indication of imperfect health." But to say that all overweight persons are cutting their lives short and will die of heart disease is ridiculous. Winston Churchill, Bismarck, Dr. Samuel Johnson, Pope John XXIII—all were topheavy yet lived useful, hale, and healthy lives, surviving many or most of their contemporaries.

In discussing obesity and heart disease we have to make distinctions before we can make sense. Reports from insurance companies, incomplete as they are, enable us to make some valid observations. The death rate from heart trouble among the obese is also tied to age. In this book I am primarily concerned with the 40-to-65 age group. As a word of consolation, let me say that death due to heart disease is far greater—almost 50 percent greater—among the obese in their twenties than in their sixties; and there is about 40 percent higher mortality from obesity with heart disease among those in their twenties as compared with those in their forties. Deaths from heart disease among overweight women are far less than among men—an unsolved mystery.

When speaking of obesity we must make the distinction between the grossly overweight and those with varying degrees of obesity on a lesser and more common level. We all recognize the grossly obese; they are not too com-

mon, but from a medical standpoint they have a invari-
ably high rate of heart disease.

An analysis of the available statistics confirms that
the incidence of heart disease increases gradually in people
5 to 10 percent overweight. The rate climbs steadily and
progressively for those 16 to 24 percent overweight, and
over the 25 percent mark it becomes prevalent.

While we have much to discover on the relationship
between overweight and heart trouble, we have more than
enough evidence to establish a connection. Apart from the
difficulties which obesity poses in the prevention or treatment of other ailments, such as peptic ulcer or diabetes,
it is a "heart factor." There is an old wives' tale that the
fatter the man, the happier his life. He had better enjoy
his days, for the odds are that they will be shorter in
number than those of people carrying less weight.

As yet, there is no absolute proof of a definite cause-
and-effect relationship between overweight and heart disease. But there is substantial evidence that extra weight
is a contributing factor, and it certainly retards treatment.

The definite cause or causes of arteriosclerosis are
unknown, although prolonged research indicates several
contributing, if not basically causative, factors. Arteriosclerosis occurs when the inner and middle linings of an
artery lose their elasticity and become clogged or thick-
ened by an accumulation of cholesterol, fats, fat pigments,
iron and calcium deposits. Why this happens we don't
know. But most American adults have a touch of arteriosclerosis in some form or other. When the heart arteries
harden, the result is frequently angina pectoris (pain in
the heart region), which is a warning signal that the
arteries are clogging. When the arteries of the brain

harden, this opens the way to a stroke. A patient who develops high blood pressure increases the peripheral resistance of his arteries as there is a loss of elasticity; in other words the normal flow of the blood meets increased resistance as it flows through the arteries.

There are some mysteries connected with coronary arteriosclerosis (which damages the coronary arteries). One is the fact that women are less affected by coronary heart disease than men. However autopsies prove that general arteriosclerosis (occurring in other arteries) is as prevalent among women as among men.

The greater incidence of high blood pressure among overweight subjects in middle years is an established fact. This is aggravated by the excess weight, which puts an added strain on the normal flow of blood through the body, and it is known that those with chronic high blood pressure are more susceptible to heart attacks.

In probing the relationship between heart trouble and overweight in middle life, the medical researcher is like a soldier in jungle warfare who feels that snipers are around. He is cautious and suspicious, and alert for the least sign of danger. He is sure that there is more than a minor connection between heart trouble and overweight in some patients, since elementary experience proves beyond question that gross overweight precipitates heart trouble. But he cannot establish yet whether or not the overweight is a direct cause in the hardening of the arteries.

For the overweight middle-ager, the following suggestions will prove valuable.

1. If you have a family history of heart disease, look

out! There is no absolute proof of hereditary tendencies in heart disease, but practical experience has shown that the hereditary factor in heart trouble is rather prevalent. Don't ignore it. Go for regular checkups. Don't decide on reducing diets without medical advice, and don't ask for dietary advice without reminding the doctor of your family's heart history.

2. Be cautious on heavy fat and sugar diets. If you are really interested in reducing you should already be wary. But also recent research indicates that the majority of overweight heart patients are careless in their nutritional habits.

3. The role of stress and strain in heart disease is also uncharted. But, when dealing with a stress-and-overweight problem, a doctor usually worries about possible heart disease. Relax—and when your work gets you down, remember that worry solves nothing. Tackling a weight problem is difficult, but if it is allied to a stress problem, heart trouble is very often around the corner.

An overweight heart patient has a double problem. Not only must he limit the strain on his heart, but he must also shed weight. Until recently the doctors had to rely almost entirely on a stringent diet, which reduced the overall fat intake. Such diets usually proved unpalatable. But two recently developed drugs, Atromid-S and Choloxin, have opened a new horizon. After careful research and testing it has been proved that these drugs, which produce no serious side effects, can in most instances reduce the cholesterol and fat content of the blood by 7 to 35 percent. This breakthrough enables your doctor to prescribe a more palatable and less stringent diet to achieve the same or better results for cholesterol problems. In 90 percent of all cases observed, these drugs were definitely beneficial in a planned, but not too severe, dieting regimen prescribed for those with high cholesterol blood levels.

CHAPTER FIFTEEN

Overweight and Diabetes

Doctors are well aware of the incidence of diabetes in overweight patients, especially in the over-40 group. Experts such as Dr. E. R. Joslin indicate that over 75 percent of all diabetic patients have had a weight problem at some stage of their life. For our present purpose, it is sufficient to bear in mind that over 60 percent of all diabetics between the ages of 40 and 65 have a weight problem.

Diabetes is a physiologic imbalance or debility which prevents a person's body from breaking down and absorbing his carbohydrate intake. The capacity of the pancreas to provide insulin to transform carbohydrate into energy becomes impaired in some measure.

The average overweight person's diet is usually top-heavy in carbohydrates and low in protein, and, unless this imbalance is remedied, it may well put too great a strain on the body's capacity to handle and transform the carbohydrate—thus paving the way for diabetes.

When the patient is overweight and "progresses" to diabetes this is what happens: his intake of carbohydrates over a period of time produces a large, poorly muscled physique; his capacity to handle carbohydrates lowers, and diabetes occurs. Prognosis for an obese patient with diabetes is far less favorable than for a patient with diabetes alone. It is known that there is often some hereditary factor in the development of diabetes; if people with a family history of diabetes tend toward overweight and do not remedy it, there is a good chance that at some stage of middle life they will themselves develop diabetes. The death rate for an overweight diabetic is 2.5 times higher than for the average middle-aged overweight person.

There are several treatments for diabetes: pills such as Orinase, Diabinese, and Dymelor; the injection of insulin to make up for the body's inability to supply it; and, of course, the strict regulation of carbohydrate intake. For the overweight diabetic, reducing is not only desirable, it is imperative. A reducing program can accomplish two things: it can remedy the weight problem and, at the same time, cure the diabetic condition.

A scientific research study was made of 35 middle-aged diabetics. Of this group, 21 followed a strict dieting program and reduced to normal weight, while 14—acting as a control group—did not follow strict dieting. Their diabetic disorders quickly vanished, and a follow-up showed that once they controlled their weight they could eat anything they wished without the reappearance of diabetic symptoms such as sugar in the urine (which is called glycosuria). One patient reverted to a badly balanced diet and put on weight, and her diabetic trouble recurred. But when she reduced, it disappeared again. Other surveys showed that a diabetic condition could improve radically as soon as there was any significant reduction of weight. Patients who have lost weight can often completely drop the use of insulin, which before the reduction was essential to their health.

The advent of diabetes is always unwelcome, but sometimes it is the stimulus that makes a food-loving overweight patient make serious efforts to reduce. Even though oral diabetic pills can improve the patient's diabetic state, there is a surer and a better way: reduce.

Although diabetes in overweight children does not respond to weight reduction in the same way, studies suggest that when an overweight adult develops diabetes the reason is his excessive intake of carbohydrates. These overwork and debilitate his body's sugar-handling mechanism.

The treatment of an overweight diabetic centers around two basic principles.

1. A sharp reduction of carbohydrate intake, which will give the body a chance to get the carbohydrate mechanism back into shape.
2. The adoption of a diet which is low in total calories and enables the body to reduce.

The direct and indirect consequences of these measures enable the diabetic to return to normal metabolic functioning.

CHAPTER SIXTEEN

Overweight and Other Middle-Age Ailments

A doctor must have coined the phrase "it is easier to give advice than to follow it." Many times I, and most doctors, have seen problems develop into tragedies because patients refused to follow advice. We try to persuade, but I believe it is naive and dishonest to cure through fear. After all, we doctors walk in the twilight of discovery; we have few mathematical proofs, but the basis for our conclusions—like belief or disbelief in God—stems from our individual and collective experience. And experience has shown us that obesity has an adverse bearing on many middle-age health problems, even though it is certainly not the main factor in most of them.

THE PEPTIC ULCER

In a previous book, *Your Ulcer: Prevention, Control, Cure,* I pointed out that ulcer incidence is greater among overweight people. But there is no proof that overweight is a causative ulcer factor. Nevertheless the ulcer patient who is overweight has a diet problem. Milk is part of ulcer therapy, but it is detrimental to a patient with a weight problem. Also, surgery on an overweight patient creates many difficulties, and healing is slow.

LIVER

Cirrhosis of the liver is more frequent in overweight patients, possibly due to maladjusted diet—high carbohydrate, low thiamine (vitamin B_1), low protein. Once an overweight man or woman develops cirrhosis, the possibility of controlling or curing the ailment is greatly reduced, apparently because of factors, as yet undetermined, connected with his or her excess weight. This phenomenon is particularly noticed in middle age. But there are no grounds for stating that overweight causes liver trouble.

GALLSTONES

The incidence of gallstones in obese men and women is slightly higher than for those of normal weight. This is not a major ailment, but, as every surgeon knows, the removal of gallstones becomes a little more difficult and dangerous in an overweight subject. The surgeon has to cut through a layer of fat three or four inches deep. And postoperative lung and abdominal complications are more frequent. However, excess weight cannot be shown to have a relationship to the genesis of gallstones.

THYROID

Some years ago researchers attempted to link overweight to subnormal thyroid activity. But the underactivity of the thyroid gland is not related to overweight nor is the converse true. Patients with myxedema (very low activity of the thyroid) sometimes develop increased weight, but that extra weight is not due to fat deposits but rather to an excessive storage of water and a malfunction of the water disposal mechanism of the body. Overweight patients have no more thyroid trouble than any other group.

In these and in a host of ailments common in middle years, ranging from pulmonary diseases to endocrine disorders, there is no causative relationship between overweight and the disease. But there is no doubt that excessive weight retards treatment and recovery.

CHAPTER SEVENTEEN

Overweight, Drugs, and Formula Diets

A person who decides to battle overweight and shed unwanted pounds quickly finds that he must do so alone.

Unless he is grossly obese, his friends and most of his relatives are rarely interested in his problem, which they feel is of minor importance. For the most part they are not concerned—unless his dieting or reducing program causes them some inconvenience.

DIET DRUGS

Those who have a weight problem hope and dream that some day a shortcut program will arrive, perhaps a pill which will offer a quick, painless, and sure solution! An endless flow of brand-named drugs continually buoy the hopes of the public, but as yet there is no drug available which answers the hopes of the overweight. Some drugs, taken under strict medical supervision, can help a person to reduce, but by themselves they cannot solve the problem. One could fill a book describing such drugs, but for our purpose, we will discuss only the principal "drug approaches."

Amphetamines and a multitude of related drugs have anorexic properties: they inhibit or depress hunger pangs and cause a loss of appetite. Doctors prescribe their use for some patients, but, for many cogent reasons, they are not enthusiastic about their general use. About one-third of patients taking amphetamines experience some undesirable side effects: palpitation of the heart, increased nervousness, and varied gastrointestinal disorders. To lessen nervous side effects, some of these drugs are combined with sedatives. Of course they cannot be given to people with heart trouble, nervous ailments, or high blood pressure. Under medical supervision they can be a help, for a short time. But since they are habit-forming, their use can, and often does, create a problem rather than solve one. Whatever good such products accomplish is short-lived. When the doctor decides for nutritional or other reasons to discontinue the use of such drugs, the patient very quickly realizes that unless he is willing to follow a dietary regimen the good effects of the drugs are very transitory.

If a person decides to diet he should be prepared to suffer mild withdrawal symptoms: increased tension, emotional stress, restlessness, and perhaps depression. For that reason the use of sedatives can then be most helpful. Many doctors recommend phenobarbital before meals. However the prolonged use of sedatives is neither recommended nor desirable.

Today few doctors are inclined to recommend vegetable non-metabolized gums such as methycellulose. Products like Melozets temporarily curb the appetite, and give a false feeling of satiety. Taken in wafer or in *other* forms, they swell or bulk in the stomach when the person drinks water. Few people have, in the long run, benefited from such products; over a length of time these products can create some nutritional problems.

The heavy use of laxatives to cut down on the absorption of food by speeding its exit through the intestines is useless in weight therapy. Coated foods which are supposed to achieve the same result are equally futile. A more radical solution—cutting out most of the small bowel to reduce food absorption—is a foolish and dangerous experiment which can never be recommended.

In the middle years the use of drugs or miracle methods should, for the most part, be avoided in a reducing program. Yet women rarely follow this advice. Being more weight-conscious than men, they are also more willing to follow any random diet advice they get. Doctors constantly hear the typical story: "A friend of mine took a new drug . . . why don't you give it to me?" Men and women in middle years will benefit more from following their doctors' advice than by hoping for a weight solution from drugs or shortcut therapy.

FORMULA DIETS

There is hardly an overweight middle-ager around who hasn't heard of or used a formula diet. For over 12 years they have been widely, but not enthusiastically, used. (You never heard of a man raising a rumpus because his formula diet wasn't on the table when he arrived home from work!) Today manufacturers are attempting to make their formula diets more tempting, marketing them in various flavors with the verve of ice cream dealers.

The most popular brands are household words—Metrecal, which is available in liquid, powder, and solid form; Nutrament, which is sold in liquid and powder form. Basically these, and other similar products, are prepared to enable the dieter to cut down his caloric intake to about 900 calories a day. They contain, in balanced ratios, protein from milk or soy flour, fats, and carbohydrates, together with vitamins and minerals equal to the established daily requirements.

Such products are effective and safe and can be used without medical supervision except by those with heart, kidney, or diabetic ailments. These are low residue (non-bulky) diets and should be supplemented with high residue foods such as lettuce or celery, otherwise those using them will develop constipation.

These reducing diets have great adjunctive value in weight therapy. Their drawback is that they become monotonous, and few people can abide such regimens for a long time. Doctors don't recommend them for the three meals a day. It is far better for a person to use them in place of lunch or dinner for a given period. Some dieters skip breakfast or lunch altogether. I don't think this is a good idea, and I advise such people to substitute one of these packaged diets.

While complete diet products can help a middle-ager to drop some pounds, their effectiveness is short-lived unless the person resolves to follow a controlled diet. There is no once-forever method of reducing: it is a continuous job requiring determination and culinary self-education.

How Not to Regain Lost Weight

When in middle age you lose unwanted weight you experience a rewarding sense of psychological and physical achievement. But you should realize that while you have won a major battle, the war is not over. Yet, you may say, you can hardly be expected to live interminably on a rigid diet! No, but you have to make up your mind that all your good work will be easily undone unless you make a determined resolution to follow some tested general principles.

1. Protein foods can be eaten in quantity and should never drop below the level of the reduction diet.
2. Fruits and vegetables can be eaten in any desired quantity; for dessert you should foster the habit of eating fruit instead of pastries, ice cream, or other rich foods.
3. Sugars should be used sparingly or not at all.
4. Avoid second helpings of heavy gravies and do not cover vegetables with butter or rich sauces.

5. Cut down on snacks between meals and if possible avoid them altogether.
6. If you need a drink to relax before dinner, limit yourself to one but do not make it as big as the normal three. Measure your drink if you have a heavy hand; otherwise you will succumb to the temptation of being overgenerous to yourself.
7. Exercise daily, and try to choose an outdoor exercise that suits you. In bad weather when this is impossible, substitute some exercise such as push-ups at home.
8. Don't become too faddish about your weight. Get on the scales once a week at a particular hour of a certain day—for instance, before breakfast on Saturday.
9. Develop an interest in food and read the recipes in your daily paper. Most days you will find something that is permissible and you might as well get the last ounce of enjoyment out of the food that won't put on weight.
10. Avoid tension, because you might possibly try to salve your trouble with a few extra drinks or a big meal.
11. Remember that the method of food preparation makes a caloric difference—broiled, roasted, or baked foods are preferable to fried foods.

Keeping your weight down is a problem which you alone can handle. A doctor or any book can only tender advice. You can keep trim once you have convinced yourself that it's worth the continuous dietary vigilance and effort.

CHAPTER NINETEEN

The Nutritional Value of Essential Foods

We need to know some elementary nutritional facts about the foods we eat. Some foods have been basic to the human diet for centuries. Men have always known what was nourishing, but now modern science has delineated and specified nutritive value of various types of food.

One point should be remembered: foods are of biologic origin and are, of course, subject to genetic and climatic variations. Their nutritional value is also affected by storage, processing, and method of cooking. So any statement on the value of a particular food is necessarily variable.

In our Western civilization no good meal is complete without meat. It plays a valuable role in the sustenance of human life. It has many constituent elements: iron, potassium, sodium and, most important, protein. In the average piece of meat we find 20 to 23 percent protein—and 60 percent water! Muscle meat such as steak, while less nutritive than organ meat, also contains moderate amounts of vitamins such as thiamine (vitamin B_1) and riboflavin (vitamin B_2), and a generous percentage of niacin (nicotinic acid) and phosphorus.

Organ meats, such as heart, liver, and kidney, provide protein of a very high quality, particularly all the B complex vitamins and large quantities of vitamin A.

The fat value in meats depends on the nutritional state of the animal and the trimming and cooking method adopted. In most meats the fat can easily be trimmed off, and usually is, except in pork, whose fat is interspersed throughout the muscle fibers and consequently cannot be segregated. Fat makes meat more difficult to digest; that is why pork is one of the least digestible of meats.

Poultry and game do not differ much in composition from other meats; neither do the dark and white meats of poultry differ much. But usually white meat is more digestible—it contains a little more niacin and less fat.

Many people regard fish as nutritionally inferior to meat. In fact fish and meat rank together from a nutritive viewpoint. On the whole, fish contains less fat and more water than meat. Crab and fat fish—salmon, shad, etc.—are as wholesome and digestible as fat meat or poultry; lean shellfish—such as clams—is as easily digested as good lean beef.

Cereals are worldwide food staples. Wheat and rice are the most used, followed by corn, then rye, barley, millet, and oats. These are used in either their natural form or in a processed form. Processing lowers the nutritional content of any cereal; when wheat is milled to flour some of the mineral and vitamin content is lost. Today this loss is compensated for by the addition of "enrichments": riboflavin, niacin, iron, thiamine. Common breakfast cereals, precooked for easy use, benefit greatly by enrichment and the addition of elements lost in their preparation.

Vegetables are dominated by the potato family. The white potato is a staple item in the European and American diet. Its prime nutritive element is carbohydrate—20 percent in every potato. The protein value of the potato is slight—just 2 percent in the case of a poor biologic protein type.

Leafy vegetables are not energy-yielding. Lettuce and cabbage are low in carbohydrate, high in minerals and vitamins. Such foods provide roughage which is helpful to a balanced diet. The greener the vegetable the more carotene (preformed vitamin A) it has and the greater its nutritional value.

The most common diet fruit is the tomato (which is commonly regarded as a vegetable). It is rich in vitamins A and C. When canned, the tomato retains much of its vitamin C, losing less of its nutritive value than canned fruits.

Most fruits do not contribute essentially to the protein or calorie content of any diet. Their value lies in their vitamin and mineral content. Oranges or orange juice contribute valuable quantities of vitamin C.

Eggs contain 13 percent protein, 12 percent fat, and a little carbohydrate. The egg yolk is more essential than the white: it contains most of the vitamins.

Milk is a rich food, high in protein, calcium, riboflavin, and vitamin A, lactose (milk sugar), and milk fat. Casein is the major milk protein. The nutritive value of cow's milk depends in some measure on the feed of the cow. Milk is poor in iron and vitamin C. Evaporated or powdered milk retains most of its nutritive value and loses some of its fat content.

Milk products such as cheese are nutritionally valuable. Cheese contains all the protein and some of the minerals of the milk from which it is made.

These general remarks show that the nutritional components of various foods are as varied as people. In the second part of the book is more specific information in the form of a calorie rundown of the most common foods and drinks.

CHAPTER TWENTY

An Approach to Dieting

In childhood and right through life we develop tastes for various foods, and we rarely realize how limited those tastes are. When we go dieting we discover that some of our favorite dishes are taboo from a weight point of view. And consequently dieting becomes an involuntary penance, something of a chore which we would like to finish as soon as possible.

However, it is never too late to learn, and dieters should make a concerted effort to discover new foods and new ways of preparing food, and to savor the great pleasure of finding a low-calorie dish which they enjoy. Variety lightens the burden of dieting.

SIMPLE RULES FOR DIETERS

1. Try to learn what foods are low-calorie.
2. Plan your meals, or a program of meals, in advance. Vary your low-calorie menu.
3. In every daily menu include: citrus fruit; meat

or fish or poultry or cheese; eggs; skimmed milk; two vegetables.

4. Don't load your refrigerator. Buy, or ask your wife to buy, only what is needed for two days' meals. A well-stocked refrigerator is a temptation to break a dieting program.

5. Vary your foods, and eat small portions.

6. If possible skip between-meal snacks. If you snack, treat the calorie intake as part of your daily allowance.

7. Eat slowly, avoid second helpings, and stick to a low-calorie dessert.

9. Don't add salt to your food after it is cooked.

10. Drink 6 to 8 glasses of fluids daily.

11. Get sufficient sleep each night and never neglect daily exercise.

12. If you suffer from any illness, do not diet without the advice of your doctor.

13. Avoid the dangerous fad of "starvation" diets.

14. Remember there are no miracle cures for overweight. Follow professional advice and you will lose weight.

PLANNED DIETING

As I said in early chapters of this book the middle-ager has to battle against overweight. A plan is needed, for spasmodic assaults on diet give very little long-distance benefit. A word on the diet section which follows:

The first step is to educate yourself on the specific values of various foods and beverages. These are given in the Appendixes to this book. It is most helpful to know both calorie content and carbohydrate, protein, and fat values of common foods if you wish to approach your reducing program intelligently.

The second step is to study the eight diet programs which follow. In fact, all that has been written so far merely serves as a preface to the diets, an attempt to make dieting meaningful and more viable. The eight programs are balanced and varied. And while all can be used beneficially by any overweight person, each diet has side benefits for those with a particular ailment apart from their overweight.

Each of the eight diets provides for all nutritional needs and is guaranteed to enable you to lose two or three pounds weekly.

PART TWO

THE EIGHT REDUCING DIETS

Notes: 1 glass or 1 cup = 8 oz.

A sugar substitute is always permissible when *no sugar* is called for. Also, a sugar substitute is permitted whenever *sugar* is called for. Skim milk may be used with coffee or tea anytime.

DIET I

Suitable for all but especially for those with diabetes or high blood pressure.

SAMPLE MENUS

MONDAY

Breakfast
> Grapefruit, ½ small
> Dry cereal, ½ cup (sugar substitute, if desired)
> Skim milk, ½ cup
> Coffee or tea (no sugar)

Lunch
> Tomato stuffed with chicken: use 1 tomato,
>   ½ cup diced chicken, 1 tsp. mayonnaise, capers, parsley,
>   celery, lettuce
> Whole wheat bread, 1 slice
> Margarine, 1 pat
> Coffee or tea (no sugar)

Dinner

Baked fish filet, 4 oz.
Tossed green salad, generous serving low-calorie dressing
Asparagus, ½ cup
Baked potato, 1 medium
Butter or margarine, 1 pat
Fresh or canned pear, 1
Coffee or tea (no sugar)

A sugar substitute is always permissible when *no sugar* is called for. Skim milk may be used with coffee or tea.
Coffee or tea (no sugar)

TUESDAY

Breakfast

Orange juice, ½ cup
Egg, 1, poached or soft-boiled, on 1 slice toast
Coffee or tea (no sugar)

Lunch

Veal, 4 oz.
Coleslaw, 1 serving
Green beans, 1 serving
Sour pickle, 1
Rye bread, 1 slice
Butter or margarine, 1 pat
Skim milk, 1 glass; or coffee or tea (no sugar)

Dinner

Roast leg lamb, 4 oz.
Corn, 1 small ear
Butter or margarine, ½ pat
Carrots and peas, ½ cup
Strawberries, fresh or frozen, 1 cup
Coffee or tea (no sugar)

WEDNESDAY

Breakfast
> Tomato juice, ½ cup
> Oatmeal, ½ cup (1 tsp. sugar)
> Skim milk, ½ cup
> Coffee or tea (no sugar)

Lunch
> Open roast beef sandwich, 3 oz. beef (2 thin slices)
> Rye or whole wheat bread, 1 slice
> Butter or margarine, 1 pat
> Canned tomatoes, ½ cup
> Tossed salad (all you desire)
> Coffee or tea (no sugar)

Dinner
> Flounder, baked or broiled, 4 oz.
> Lettuce, 1 large serving, low-calorie dressing
> Broccoli, 1 serving
> Carrot, 1 raw
> Strawberries or blueberries, ½ cup
> Skim milk, ½ cup
> Coffee or tea (no sugar)

THURSDAY

Breakfast
> Grapefruit juice, ½ cup
> Cereal (ready-to-eat), ¾ cup (1 tsp. sugar)
> Skim milk, ½ cup
> Coffee or tea (no sugar)

Lunch
> Shrimp salad, 3 oz.
> Boiled potato, 1 small
> Enriched white bread, 1 slice
> Butter or margarine, 1 pat
> Coffee or tea (no sugar)

Dinner
Turkey, 4 oz.
Mixed green salad (all you desire)
Spinach, 1 serving
Whole wheat bread, ½ slice
Butter or margarine, ½ pat
Strawberries or blackberries, ½ cup
Coffee or tea (no sugar)

FRIDAY

Breakfast
Orange juice, ½ cup
Egg, 1, poached or soft-boiled
Rye bread, 1 slice
Butter or margarine, ½ pat
Coffee or tea (no sugar)

Lunch
Baked flounder, 4 oz.
Potato, boiled or baked, 1 small
Butter or margarine, 1 pat
Cauliflower, 1 serving
Carrots, 2 raw
Coffee or tea (no sugar)

Dinner
Roast chicken, leg and thigh
Green beans, 1 serving
Head lettuce, wedge, with lemon
Pear, 1 small
Skim milk, 1 glass

SATURDAY

Breakfast
Cantaloupe, ½ medium
Cereal (ready-to-eat) ¾ cup (1 tsp. sugar)
Skim milk, ½ cup
Coffee or tea (no sugar)

Lunch

Luncheon meat, 2 slices
American cheese, 1 slice
Lettuce, generous serving
Whole wheat bread, 1 slice
Butter or margarine, 1 pat
Peach, 1 medium
Skim milk, 1 glass, or coffee or tea (no sugar)

Dinner

Baked halibut, 4 oz.
Potato, boiled or baked, 1 medium
Butter or margarine, 1 pat
Tossed salad, all you desire
Honeydew melon, ¼ small
Coffee or tea (no sugar)

SUNDAY

Breakfast

Orange, 1 small
Egg, 1, poached or soft-boiled, on 1 slice toast
Butter or margarine, ½ pat
Skim milk, 1 glass

Lunch

Liver, broiled, with sautéed onion and mushrooms, 4 oz.
Asparagus, ½ cup
Mashed potatoes, 1 serving
Butter or margarine, 1 pat
Tossed green salad (all you desire), low-calorie dressing
Pineapple, ½ cup
Coffee or tea (no sugar)

Dinner

Baked codfish, 4 oz.
Broccoli, 1 generous serving
Mixed green salad, all you desire
Sherbet, ½ cup
Coffee or tea (no sugar)

SUGGESTED VARIATIONS

Meat, Poultry, and Fish   Chicken, turkey, veal, fish (4-oz. servings) in most of your meals for the week. Lean beef, lamb, pork, and ham (4-oz. servings) in no more than 5 meals per week. Liver (4 oz.) once a week only. Luncheon meat and cheese (3 to 4 oz.) once weekly.

MEAT CHOICES: lean ground, lean cuts. Trim all visible fat before cooking.

MEAT PREPARATION: bake, broil, roast, or stew so that you can discard the fat which cooks out of the meat.

Shellfish   Clams, crab, lobster, oysters, scallops, shrimp.

Eggs   No more than 3 weekly, never fried.

Milk   Skim milk only, 1 glass (8 oz.) once or twice daily.

Bread   Whole wheat, rye, oatmeal, pumpernickel, enriched white, not more than 2 slices daily.

Cereal   1 serving (½ cup), hot or cold, 4 servings weekly.

Butter or margarine   No more than 10 pats weekly.

Fluids   6 to 8 glasses daily.

Salt   Just enough to make food palatable.

Vegetables   Eat as many raw vegetables as you desire. If cooked, limit amount to ½ cup: asparagus, green beans, beet greens, broccoli, cabbage, cauliflower, carrots, celery, cucumber, endive, escarole, kale, lettuce, mushrooms, pimentos, radishes, rhubarb, sauerkraut, spinach, squash, tomatoes, turnips, watercress.

Fruit (fresh or unsweetened)   ½ cup serving once or twice daily: applesauce, blackberries, blueberries, grapes, grapefruit juice*, orange juice*, pineapple, pineapple juice, raspberries, 1 small apple, ½ medium cantaloupe, ½ medium grapefruit*, ¼ small honeydew, 1 small orange*, 1 medium peach, 1 small pear, 1 medium plum, 1 cup strawberries*, 1 medium tangerine, watermelon (½ slice, 1-inch-thick).

* High in vitamin C, and can be used interchangeably. Use once daily.

FOODS TO AVOID

These meats should be avoided or used sparingly: duck and goose; organ meats (liver once weekly, kidney, heart, sweetbreads); heavily marbled and fatty meats; spareribs, frankfurters, sausages, fatty hamburgers, bacon, luncheon meats, mutton.

Fresh dates and figs, and all dried fruits.

Avocados, and olives.

Whole milk and whole milk products: chocolate milk; canned whole milk; ice cream; all creams including sour, half and half, whipped; whole milk yogurt; and non-dairy cream substitutes.

Butter rolls, biscuits, muffins, doughnuts, pies, cookies, crackers, nuts, egg bread, cheese bread.

Sauces, commercial mixes containing dried eggs, egg yolks, and whole milk.

Potatoe chips and all deep fried snacks.

Puddings.

Peanut butter, jelly, jam, marmalade, honey.

Candy and soft drinks.

FLAVOR AIDS FOR VARIED MEALS

Try basil, rosemary, garlic salt, dry mustard, or curry with beef or lamb; rosemary or savory with veal, chicken, or fish.

Season tomatoes with curry, basil, or oregano; turnips with rosemary; cabbage with savory; carrots or zucchini with thyme or nutmeg; cauliflower with dill; spinach with marjoram.

DIET II

Suitable for all but especially for women with
irregular periods and other menstrual problems.

SAMPLE MENUS

Breakfast
 Grapefruit, ½ small
 Egg, 1, poached or soft-boiled
 Whole wheat bread, 1 slice, plain or toasted
 Butter or margarine, 1 pat
 Skim milk, 1 glass
 Coffee or tea (no sugar)

Lunch
 Oysters (raw), 10 medium; or tuna fish (canned), 4 oz.
 Lima beans (green), ½ cup
 Brussels sprouts, ½ cup
 Whole wheat or enriched white bread, 1 slice
 Butter or margarine, ½ pat
 Skim milk, 1 small glass (6 oz.)

Dinner

Roast chicken, 4 oz.
Broccoli, ½ cup; or green peas, ½ cup
Tossed green salad (all you desire), low-calorie dressing
Whole wheat or enriched white bread, 1 slice
Butter or margarine, ½ pat
Strawberries, ½ cup
Coffee or tea (no sugar)

Breakfast

Orange juice, ½ cup
Oatmeal, ½ cup; or cornflakes, ¾ cup (1 tsp. sugar)
Skim milk, 1 glass
Coffee or tea (no sugar)

Lunch

Crabmeat or tuna fish (canned), 4 oz.
Salad, 1 large serving
Whole wheat bread, 1 slice
Butter or margarine, 1 pat
Coffee or tea (no sugar)

Dinner

Broiled beef patties, 2 large
Asparagus, ½ cup
Tossed green salad (all you desire), vinegar dressing
Peach, 1 medium
Coffee or tea (no sugar)

SUGGESTED VARIATIONS

Meat, Poultry, Fish   Eat 4 servings (4 oz. each) of chicken or
turkey each week; fish, 5 servings weekly; lean meats 4 servings weekly; oysters, 1 serving a week. Do not fry meats,
poultry, or fish. You may substitute a serving (4 oz.) of cream
cheese or yogurt for meat courses.

Eggs   3 weekly, never fried.

Milk   Skim milk, 2 glasses daily.

Bread   Whole wheat, oatmeal, or rye, 1 or 2 slices daily.

Cereal   Oatmeal, farina, or ready-to-eat cereals, ½ cup.
Butter or margarine   1 to 2 pats daily.
Fluids   6 to 8 glasses daily.
Salt   Just enough to make food palatable.
Vegetables   Eat as many raw vegetables as desired. If they are cooked, limit amount to ½ cup: asparagus, green beans, broccoli, cabbage, carrots, cauliflower, celery, cucumber, greens, kale, lettuce, squash, spinach, tomatoes, turnips.
Fruit   Eat 1 citrus fruit daily; or ½ cup orange or tomato juice, half grapefruit. If desired, 1 serving of any fruit except bananas, dates, figs.
Iron vitamin tablet   1 daily.

FOODS TO AVOID

Salty or smoked food: anchovies, caviar, salted cod, herring, sardines.

Fruits canned or frozen in sugar syrup.

All sugar-coated cereals, pastries, cakes, sweet rolls, cookies.

Ice cream, nuts, party spreads, dips, cocoa, custards, puddings, tapioca.

Sugar—not more than 2 tsps. daily. Try to substitute a sugar substitute for sugar.

DIET III

*Suitable for all but especially for ulcer patients
and those with frequent stomach upsets.*

SAMPLE MENUS

Breakfast

Orange or grapefruit juice, ½ glass
Egg, 1, poached or soft-boiled
Enriched white bread, 1 slice plain or toasted
Butter or margarine, 1 pat
Caffeine-free coffee or weak tea (no sugar); or skim milk,
1 small glass (6 oz.)

Lunch

Baked fish filet, 4 oz.
Potato, any way but fried, 1 small
Spinach, ½ cup
Enriched white bread, 1 slice
Butter or margarine, 1 pat
Caffeine-free coffee or weak tea (no sugar)

Dinner

    Broiled lamb chop, 1
    Tender lettuce, 1 serving, low-calorie dressing
    Enriched white bread, 1 slice
    Butter or margarine, ½ pat
    Fresh strawberries, 1 cup
    Skim milk, 1 small glass (6 oz.)

Bedtime

    Angel food cake, 1 small serving

Breakfast

    Tomato juice, ½ cup
    Oatmeal, ½ cup (1 tsp. sugar)
    Skim milk, 1 glass
    Caffeine-free coffee, 1 cup (no sugar)

Lunch

    Sweetbreads, baked or broiled, 4 oz.
    Enriched white bread, 1 slice
    Butter or margarine, 1 pat
    Strawberries, ½ cup
    Skim milk, ½ cup

Dinner

    Chicken (white meat), baked or broiled, 5 oz.
    Potato, mashed, 1 serving
    Spinach, ½ cup
    Jello, 1 serving
    Skim milk, 1 glass; or caffeine-free coffee, 1 cup (no sugar)

Bedtime

    Custard, 1 serving

SUGGESTED VARIATIONS

Meat, Poultry, Fish   Beef, lamb, veal, chicken, turkey, fish, 4-oz. servings, twice daily. Must be boiled, roasted, or broiled.

Eggs   3 per week, any way but fried.

Milk products   Cottage or cream cheese, 4-oz. serving, instead of meat or fish.

Breads, Cereals   All refined cereals, ½ cup, as cream of wheat, farina, cream of rice, oatmeal, corn flakes, puffed rice, rice flakes; ½ cup noodles, spaghetti, macaroni; enriched white bread, 2 slices daily.

Salt, Condiments   Just enough salt to make food palatable. Use condiments sparingly.

Desserts   Sherbets, ices, angel food cake, sponge cake. Not more than one small serving twice weekly.

Vegetables   Eat leafy green and yellow vegetables daily. These should be cooked not raw, except lettuce. Half-cup each of asparagus tips, broccoli, cauliflower, beets, carrots, green beans, mushrooms, squash, tomato. Eat as much tender lettuce as desired. Eat 1 small potato three times weekly—any way but fried.

Fruit, fresh (ripe), frozen, or canned   Fruit juice (orange, grapefruit), ½ cup. Include 1 citrus fruit (orange, grapefruit or tomato daily, no sugar. Applesauce, ½ cup; canned or cooked peaches, pears, apricots, ½ cup; baked apple (no seeds, skin), 1 small; cantaloupe, ½ medium; honeydew melon, ¼ small; orange, 1 small; strawberries, 1 cup; watermelon, ½ 1-in. slice.

FOODS TO AVOID

Beef broth, beef cubes, bouillon, chicken broth.

Bacon, crab, corned beef, lobster, pork, sardines, shrimp.

Fried or greasy foods such as fried eggs; fried meats, chicken; or fish; fried vegetables, nuts, pie.

Hot or wholegrain bread: cornbread, hot biscuits, pancakes, griddle cakes, gingerbread, cracked wheat bread, whole wheat bread, coarse rye bread. Coarse wholegrain cereals: bran, branflakes, Ralston, shredded wheat.

All raw vegetables, except tender lettuce.

Cooked vegetables: cabbage family, corn on cob, kohlrabi, old beets, onions and garlic, parsnips, sauerkraut.

Raw fruits: apples, cherries, grapefruit, lemons, pineapple.

All spiced or pickled vegetables or fruits.

Spices or highly seasoned foods: catsup, chili sauce, horseradish, mustard, pickles and olives, rich gravies and stews, steak sauces, vinegar, Worcestershire sauce.

Tea; coffee; very hot, very cold, or alcoholic beverages.

DIET IV

*Suitable for all, but this high calcium–high
protein diet is especially good for those threatened
with osteomalacia (softening of bone) which
becomes more common as we get older.*

SAMPLE MENUS

Breakfast
  Egg, 1, poached or soft-boiled
  Orange juice, ½ cup
  Enriched white bread, 1 slice
  Butter or margarine, 1 pat
  Skim milk, 1 glass
  Coffee or tea (no sugar)

Lunch
  Yogurt or cream cheese, 4 oz.
  Whole wheat bread, 1 slice
  Butter, ½ pat
  Kale, ½ cup; or mustard greens, ½ cup
  Coffee or tea (no sugar) or skim milk, ½ cup

Dinner
>   Corned beef (canned), 4 oz.
>   Collard greens, ½ cup
>   Turnip greens, ½ cup
>   Fresh strawberries, ½ cup
>   Skim milk, 1 glass

Midnight Snack
>   Cheddar-type cheese, 1 oz.
>   Saltine cracker, 1

Breakfast
>   Grapefruit, ½ medium
>   Oatmeal, ½ cup (1 tsp. sugar)
>   Skim milk, ½ cup
>   Sugar, 1 teaspoonful
>   Coffee or tea (no sugar)

Lunch
>   Baked flounder, 5 oz.
>   Baked potato, 1 small
>   Dandelion greens, 1 serving
>   Butter or margarine, 1 pat
>   Skim milk, 1 glass

Dinner
>   Turkey meat, 4 oz.
>   Turnip greens, ½ cup
>   Lettuce, generous serving
>   Whole wheat bread, 1 slice
>   Butter or margarine, 1 pat
>   Blueberries, ½ cup
>   Skim milk, ½ cup
>   Coffee or tea (no sugar)

SUGGESTED VARIATIONS

Meat, Poultry, Fish   Chicken, turkey, oysters, fish, canned beef, beef, lamb, veal, 2 4-oz. servings daily, never fried. Liver, 4 oz., once weekly.

Eggs   3 weekly, not fried.

Milk, Milk Products   Skim milk, 2 to 3 glasses daily. Yogurt or cottage cheese, 3- to 4-oz. servings daily instead of meat.

Bread   Any type, 1 to 2 slices daily.

Cereal   Ready-to-eat cereal, 4 servings weekly, ½ cup each.

Butter or margarine   2 pats daily.

Beverages   Coffee, tea (no sugar).

Salt, Condiments   Enough salt to make food palatable. Condiments and flavoring to suit your taste.

Vegetables   Broccoli, dandelion greens, kale, mustard greens, turnip greens, cabbage, carrots, onions, okra, lettuce; 2 servings daily.

Fruit   Any fresh fruit, except bananas, figs, and dates; 1 serving daily plus at least 1 citrus fruit daily.

Multivitamin tablet   1 daily.

SUGGESTION

Reserve one day each week for fluids only. Skim milk (6 oz.) 4 times daily. Orange or grapefruit juice, 4 oz. daily. Water, coffee, or tea (no sugar), 3 to 6 glasses daily.

DIET V

*Suitable for all but especially for dieters
with liver or gallbladder ailments.*

SAMPLE MENUS

Breakfast
> Orange juice or grapefruit juice, 3 oz. (about ⅓ cup)
> Oatmeal, ½ cup (no sugar)
> Skim milk, ½ cup
> Coffee or tea (no sugar)

Lunch
> Lean beef, any kind, 4 oz.
> Spinach, ½ cup
> Potato, boiled or baked, 1 small
> Head lettuce, wedge, with lemon
> Enriched white bread, 1 slice
> Butter or margarine, ½ pat (if tolerated)
> Coffee or tea (no sugar)

Dinner
> Baked fish, 4 oz.
> Spinach, ½ cup
> Cooked carrots, ½ cup
> Enriched white bread, 1 slice
> Skim milk, 1 small glass (6 oz.)
> Coffee or tea (no sugar)

SUGGESTED VARIATIONS

Meat, Poultry, Fish   Any type lean meat, poultry, fish; 4 oz. twice daily, never fried.

Eggs   3 weekly if tolerated. Any way but fried.

Milk   Skim milk, 1 to 2 glasses daily.

Bread   1 to 2 slices daily, any type.

Cereal   Any type, ½ cup daily if eggs must be avoided.

Butter or margarine   2 pats daily, if tolerated.

Fluids   6 to 8 glasses daily.

Beverages   Coffee, tea (no sugar).

Salt   Enough to make food palatable.

Vegetables   ½-cup servings, 2 or 3 servings daily; from asparagus, broccoli, cauliflower, kale, lettuce, mushrooms, pimentos, spinach, green beans, watercress, peas, carrots.

Fruit   1 serving daily of any citrus fruit or juice, plus 1 serving daily from any other fruit except bananas, figs, dates.

FOODS TO AVOID

Greasy or fried foods, eggs, mayonnaise, salad dressing, cheese, pork products.

High-fat pastries rich in cream or suet.

Sauerkraut, onions, radishes, cabbage, turnips, cucumbers.

All spicy foods such as chili con carne and curry.

Vegetable fats, such as olive oil, corn oil, unless tolerated.

Try to use a sugar substitute in place of sugar.

DIET VI

*Suitable for all but especially for those
with gout or gouty arthritis.*

SAMPLE MENUS

Breakfast
> Citrus fruit juice (orange or grapefruit), ½ cup
> Egg, 1, not fried
> Enriched white bread, 1 slice
> Butter or margarine, 1 pat
> Coffee or tea (no sugar)

Lunch
> Lean meat, poultry, or fish, 3 oz., never fried
> Spinach, large serving
> Tossed green salad, 1 serving, low-calorie dressing
> Whole wheat bread, 1 slice
> Butter or margarine, ½ pat
> Skim milk, 1 glass

Dinner
> Lean meat, poultry, or fish, 4 oz. cooked, no fat or oil
> Vegetables, 2 servings, 1 raw and 1 cooked
> Any fruit, 1 serving (½ cup)
> Skim milk, 6 oz.
> Coffee or tea, (no sugar)

SUGGESTED VARIATIONS

Meat, Poultry, Fish   Chicken, turkey, veal, lamb, fish, shellfish; 4-oz. serving twice daily, never fried.

Eggs   3 weekly, never fried. If tolerated.

Milk   1 to 2 glasses skim milk daily.

Bread   1 to 2 slices daily, any type.

Cereal   Any type, ½ cup daily if eggs must be avoided.

Fluids   6 to 8 glasses daily.

Beverages   Coffee, tea (no sugar).

Vegetables   Eat all you desire of the following: broccoli, cauliflower, kale, lettuce, mushrooms, pimentos, spinach, green beans, watercress, squash, celery, tomatoes, cabbage, turnips.

Fruit   1 serving of any citrus fruit; 1 serving of any other fruit daily, except bananas, dates or figs.

FOODS TO AVOID

Meats: beef ribs, beefsteak, beef sirloin, liver, ham, mutton, sweetbreads, brains, anchovies, kidney, sardines, tripe, veal.

All fried foods.

Fish: cod, halibut, salmon.

Vegetables: asparagus, beans, onions, peameal, potatoes (but potatoes are permissible once or twice a week).

Alcoholic drinks.

SUGGESTION

If possible, reserve 1 day each week for fluids only.

DIET VII

*Suitable for all but especially for those with
"tired blood" which is an iron-deficiency anemia.*

SAMPLE MENUS

Breakfast
    Orange or grapefruit juice, ½ cup
    Egg, 1, poached or soft-boiled
    Whole wheat or rye bread, 1 slice
    Butter or margarine, 1 pat
    Coffee or tea (no sugar)

Lunch
    Oysters (raw), 10 medium
    Spinach, ½ cup
    Lima beans, ½ cup
    Whole wheat bread, 1 slice
    Strawberries, ½ cup
    Butter or margarine, 1 pat
    Coffee or tea (no sugar)

Dinner
>   Fresh liver, 4 oz., never fried
>   Cabbage, generous serving
>   Tossed green salad, generous serving, low-calorie dressing
>   Enriched white bread, 1 slice
>   Butter or margarine, 1 pat
>   Skim milk, 6 oz.
>   Coffee or tea (no sugar)

Breakfast
>   Grapefruit, ½ medium
>   Cereal (ready-to-eat), ⅔ cup (1 tsp. sugar)
>   Skim milk, ½ cup

Lunch
>   Chicken soup, 1 small cup
>   Crackers, 2
>   Turkey, 4 oz.
>   Beet greens, ½ cup
>   Cantaloupe, ¼ medium
>   Coffee or tea (no sugar)

Dinner
>   Chicken livers, 3 oz.
>   Chard, ½ cup
>   Green peas, ½ cup
>   Whole wheat bread, 1 slice
>   Butter or margarine, 1 pat
>   Skim milk, 1 glass
>   Coffee or tea (no sugar)

SUGGESTED VARIATIONS

Meat, Poultry, Fish   Liver, rich in iron, is your best bet; eat 1 3-oz. serving twice weekly. Oysters (raw) are next best; eat 2 servings weekly. Turkey, 5 oz., lean beef, any kind, 5 oz., poultry, 4 oz., baked fish, 5 oz., chicken liver, 3 oz.

Eggs   3 weekly, not fried.

Milk   Skim milk, 2 glasses daily.

Bread   Whole wheat or enriched white, 1 or 2 slices daily.

Cereal   Oatmeal, 3 times weekly. Shredded wheat once weekly.

Butter or margarine   2 pats daily.

Fluids   At least 4 to 6 glasses daily.

Beverages   Coffee, tea (no sugar).

Salt and Condiments   Just enough salt to make food palatable. Condiments and flavorings as desired.

Vegetables   Spinach, mustard greens, turnip greens, cabbage, carrots, onions, potatoes, lima beans, beet greens, chard, green peas, summer squash, corn (white or yellow). 2 servings daily.

Fruit   1 citrus fruit daily, 1 serving daily of any other fruit except bananas, dates, figs.

Iron-vitamin pills   2 daily.

DIET VIII

Suitable for all, but this 1200-calorie, proportioned
fat diet is particularly beneficial for
dieters who have had a heart attack.

CORONARY HEART DIET

No heart patient, after a heart attack, should diet without some medical advice. The diet which I give is rather basic, and covers the essentials which your doctor will possibly prescribe. The principles involved are fundamental.

1. Increase intake of low-fat products: fruits, lean meats, poultry, fish, seafoods, vegetables and vegetable oils (corn, soy, cottonseed, safflower).
2. Decrease intake of spreads, butter, cream, ice cream, cheese (except cottage), eggs, gravies, baked foods, meat fats, chocolate.
3. Do not eat more than three eggs a week, and do not have shellfish more than once. Avoid fatty meats, such as bacon, short ribs. Limit yourself to one helping of any meat per meal, but not more than three times a week.
4. Avoid, or limit, sugar, cookies, pie, jelly, candy, carbonated drinks, and liquor.

The diet will help you to lose about two and a half pounds a week, and it will also lower your cholesterol and triglyceride (fat) blood levels.

Breakfast
Citrus fruit, 1 serving
Egg, 1 (but only twice a week)
Bread, 2 slices or 1 slice toast and 1 serving cereal (List 1)
New margarine,* 1 tsp.
Skim milk, 1 cup
Coffee or tea (no sugar)

Lunch
Fish, 3 oz. (List 2A)
Oil (unsaturated), 1 tsp.
Vegetable, 1 or more serving (List 3A)
Bread, 1 slice or substitute (List 1)
Fruit, 1 serving (List 4)
Tea or coffee (no sugar)

Dinner
Very lean meat, 3 oz. (List 2B or substitute from List 2A)
Potato, 1 small; or substitute (List 1)
Vegetable, 1 or more serving (List 3A)
Vegetable, 1 serving (List 3B)
Oil (unsaturated), 2 tsp.
Fruit, 1 serving (List 4)
Coffee or tea (no sugar)

LIST 1—BREAD

The following are substitutes for 1 slice of bread.

Cereal, cooked, ½ cup
Dry cereal (puff and flake type), ¾ cup
Grits, rice, macaroni, spaghetti, ½ cup

* New margarine: high in unsaturated fatty acids (made from corn, cottonseed, soy, safflower oils)

Crackers: saltines (2-in. square), 5
   soda (2-in. square), 3
   oyster, ½ cup
   graham (2½-in. square), 2
Flour, 2½ tbs.
Matzo, ½
Melba toast, 3
Beans, peas, dried, cooked (lima, navy, split pea, etc.), ½ cup
Popcorn, popped, but not buttered, 1 cup
Potato, white, baked or boiled, 1 small
   mashed, ½ cup
Potato, sweet or yam, ¼ cup
Angel food cake, plain (1¼-in. cube), 1
Hard roll, 1

LIST 2A—PROTEIN

From this list, select fish five to six times a week, poultry
three to four times, and liver once a week.

Fish   For a 3-oz. portion, start with ¼ lb. raw weight of fresh
or frozen fish (fresh- or saltwater fish) such as: Boston blue-
fish, cod, flounder, halibut, fresh tuna, mackerel, perch, sword-
fish, salmon, trout.
    Canned fish, ¼ cup, may be substituted for 1 oz. of fresh
or frozen fish (use water-pack or drain off oil): crab, lobster,
salmon, tuna.
    3 medium sardines.
    5 small shrimp, clams, or oysters (higher in cholesterol;
limit use of these as a main dish).
Low-Fat Cottage Cheese   Eat ¼ cup in place of 1 oz. of fish
    or meat.
Peanut Butter   Use 2 tbs. instead of 1 oz. of meat or fish.
Poultry   Average serving (3 oz.) 2 or 3 times a week.
Liver   1 serving (3 oz.) may be used per week.

LIST 2B—PROTEIN

Eat no more than 1 serving (3 oz.) of cooked meat per day, or ¼ lb. (4 oz.) raw weight.

Beef   Extra lean, ground, flank, sirloin, tenderloin.
Lamb   Lean leg roast, trimmed lean chops.
Pork   trimmed ham steak, lean Canadian loin.
Veal   Plain cutlet, lean loin or rib chop, steak, or roast.
Liver   Any kind, prepared as other meats, once a week.

LIST 3A—VEGETABLES

Raw, as desired. If cooked, 1 cup.

Asparagus
Broccoli
Brussels sprouts
Cabbage
Cauliflower
Celery
Chicory
Cucumber
Eggplant
Escarole
Green beans, young
Lettuce
Mushrooms
Okra

Pepper
Radish
Sauerkraut
Summer squash
Tomato, 1 (or ½ cup juice)
Watercress
Greens:
     Beet
     Chard
     Dandelion
     Kale
     Mustard
     Spinach
     Turnip

LIST 3B—VEGETABLES

One serving is ½ cup.

Beets   Pumpkin
Carrots   Rutabaga
Onions   Squash, winter
Peas, green   Turnips

LIST 4—FRUIT

These may be fresh, dried, cooked, canned or frozen.

Apple, 1 small
Applesauce, ½ cup
Apricots, fresh, 2 medium
Apricots, canned or dried, 4 halves
Banana, ½ small
Blackberries, 1 cup
Raspberries, 1 cup
Strawberries, 1 cup
Blueberries, ⅔ cup
Cantaloupe, ¼
Cherries, 10 large
Dates, 2
Figs, fresh, 2
Figs, dried, 1 small
Grapefruit, ½ small
Grapefruit juice, ½ cup
Grapes, 12
Honeydew melon, medium, ⅛
Grape juice, ¼ cup
Mango, ¼ cup
Orange, 1 small
Orange juice, ½ cup
Papaya, ½ medium
Peach, 1 medium

Pear, 1 small
Pineapple, ½ cup
Pineapple juice, ½ cup
Plums, 2 medium
Prunes, dried, 2 medium
Raisins, 2 tbs.
Tangerine, 1 large
Watermelon, 1 cup

FLAVORINGS

You may use noncaloric food items: sugar substitutes, spices, herbs, soy sauce, meat tenderizers, Worcestershire sauce, liquid "smoke" or "charcoal" flavorings.

BEVERAGES

Clear coffee or tea without sugar or cream, club soda, or lemonade made with sugar substitute. Skim milk is permissible with coffee or tea.

APPENDIXES

Caloric Value of Foods

BEVERAGES

FOOD	APPROXIMATE AMOUNT	CALORIES
Coffee or tea, clear; sweeten with sugar substitute	1 serving cup	0
Cocoa, dry, with skim milk; sweeten with sugar substitute	1 tsp. cocoa, 1 serv. cup milk	50
Juice		
apple, canned	1 4-oz. glass	50
grapefruit	1 4-oz. glass	40
orange, fresh or frozen	1 4-oz. glass	45
orange-grapefruit blend, canned, unsweetened	1 4-oz. glass	40
pineapple, canned	1 4-oz. glass	50
tomato, canned	1 4-oz. glass	25
V-8 Cocktail	1 4-oz. glass	20
Milk, buttermilk, fat-free, or skim	1 8-oz. glass	85
Postum, instant, clear	1 cup, 1 rounded tsp.	20

BREADS, CEREALS, CRACKERS

FOOD	APPROXIMATE AMOUNT	CALORIES
Bagel, water	1	55
Bread		
cracked wheat	1 slice	60
French or Vienna	1 medium slice	55
Italian	1 small piece	55
raisin	1 slice	65
rye (American)	1 slice	55
white	1 slice	65
whole wheat	1 slice	55
Cereals °		
bran flakes, 40%	¾ cup	100
corn flakes	1 cup	100
Cream of Wheat	¾ cup	100
Grape-Nuts Flakes	1 cup	100
hominy (cooked)	1 cup	120
Kix	1 cup	100
oatmeal (cooked)	1 cup	150
Puffed Rice	1 cup	110
Puffed Wheat	1 cup	45
Rice Krispies	1 cup	110
Wheatena	⅔-cup	100
Wheaties	1 cup	105
wheat, shredded	1 large biscuit	100
Crackers		
butter	1	20
cheese, miniatures	10	15
Ritz	1	15
Ritz, cheese	1	15
Saltine	1	20
soya	1	10
Ry-Krisp	1 double	20
Triscuit	1	25

° Caloric value does not include cream, milk, or sugar.

BREADS, CEREALS, CRACKERS (cont.)

FOOD	APPROXIMATE AMOUNT	CALORIES
Doughnut, raised	1 medium	120
Muffin, bran	1 medium	105
Muffin, white or whole wheat	1 medium	120
Pancake, buckwheat or white mix	1 average 4″ diam.	65

DAIRY PRODUCTS

Butter	1 tsp.	35
Margarine	1 tsp.	35
Cottage cheese	3 level tbs.	45
Egg, poached or boiled	1 medium	80
Yogurt, plain	1 cup	120

FRUITS

Apple, fresh	1 small 2¼″ diam.	50
Applesauce, canned, unsweetened	½ cup	50
Apricots, canned, water-packed	4 halves, ½ tbs. juice	30
Blackberries, fresh	¾ cup	60
Blackberries, canned, water-packed	½ cup	50
Blueberries, canned, water-packed	½ cup	45
Cantaloupe or muskmelon	½ of 4½″ diam.	30

FRUITS (cont.)

FOOD	APPROXIMATE AMOUNT	CALORIES
Cherries, canned, water-pack	½ cup	50
Fruit cocktail, canned	6 tbs. fruit and juice	70
Grapefruit	½ small of 3¾″ diam.	40
Honeydew melon	¼ of 5″ diam.	30
Olives		
green (pickled)	3 large	20
ripe (Mission)	3 large	35
Orange, fresh	1 small 2½″ diam.	45
Peaches, canned, water-packed	2 halves, 1-2 tbs. juice	30
Peach, fresh	1 medium	45
Pear, fresh	1 medium	65
Pears, canned, water-packed	2 halves, 1 tbsp. juice	30
Pinneapple, canned, water-packed	2 small slices, 2 tbs. juice	55
Plums, fresh	2 medium	50
Prunes, dried, cooked, no sugar	4 medium, 2 tbs. juice	85
Raspberries, red, fresh	¾ cup	60
Raspberries, canned, juice-pack	½ cup scant	50
Tangerine	1 large	45
Strawberries, fresh	10 large	40

MEATS, POULTRY, FISH

FOOD	APPROXIMATE AMOUNT	CALORIES
Bacon	1 thin 6″ strip, drained	50
Beef, pot-roasted chuck	1 slice, 2″ by 1½″ by ½″	95
Beef, canned corned beef	1 slice, 3″ by 2¼″ by ¼″	65
Beef, canned corned beef hash	1 small serving, ½ cup	140
Beef, round-cut beef hamburger, no roll	1 small patty	120
Beef, rib roast	1 slice, 3″ by 2¼″ by ¼″	95
Beef, cube steak	1 piece, 4″ by 1″ by 1″	80
Beef, broiled sirloin, no bone	1 piece, 4″ by 1″ by 1″	105
Bologna	1 slice, 4½″ diam. by ⅛″	65
Frankfurter, no roll	1 average, 5½″ by ¾″ diam.	125
Ham, lean, fresh, or smoked	1 slice, 4″ by 2½″ by ⅛″	120
Ham, deviled	1 rounded tbs.	95
Ham, canned spiced	1 slice, 3¼″ by 2½″ by ¼″	125
Heart, braised beef	⅓ medium heart, with juice	130
Lamb, roasted shoulder	1 slice, 3″ by 2¾″ by ⅛″	105
Lamb, roasted leg	1 slice, 3″ by 2¾″ by ⅛″	80
Liver, beef	1 slice, 3″ by 2¼″ by ⅜″	85
Liver, calf	1 slice, 3″ by 2¼″ by ⅜″	75
Liver, chicken	1 medium-large liver	75
Liver, spread	1 rounded tbs.	50
Liverwurst	1 slice, 3″ diam. by ¼″	80
Luncheon meat	1 slice	80

MEATS, POULTRY, FISH (cont.)

FOOD	APPROXIMATE AMOUNT	CALORIES
Pork, fried chop	1 small	150
Pork, roasted loin	1 slice, 3" by 2½" by ¼"	100
Pork, roasted shoulder	1 slice, 4" by 2" by ¼"	160
Pork, roasted spareribs	meat from 3 med. ribs	125
Sausage, Vienna	2 av., 2" long by ¾" diam.	80
Veal, roasted leg	1 slice, 3" by 2" by ⅛"	70
Veal, stew with carrots	½ cup	120
Venison, cooked	1 slice, 3½" by 2½" by ¼"	80
Chicken, canned	2 tbs.	60
Chicken, fried breast	¼ of breast	115
Chicken, fried leg, no bone	1 small	65
Chicken stewed or roasted	1 slice, 3½" by 2½" by ¼"	80
Duck, roasted	1 slice, 3½" by 3" by ¼"	110
Turkey, roasted	1 slice, 3½" by 2½" by ¼"	80
Anchovies, canned	3 thin filets	20
Anchovy paste	1 tsp.	15
Clams, raw or steamed	½ dozen medium	75
Crab, canned or fresh cooked	⅝ cup meat	105
Flounder, fresh or frozen	1 piece, 3" by 3" by ½"	70
Lobster, canned	⅔ cup meat	90
Lobster paste	1 tsp.	15
Oysters, raw	½ dozen medium	80
Perch, fried filet	1 2⅔-oz. serving	110

MEATS, POULTRY, FISH (cont.)

FOOD	APPROXIMATE AMOUNT	CALORIES
Salmon, smoked	2 to 3 small slices	90
Shrimp, canned, drained	5 medium	65

SALADS

Apple, celery, walnuts, mayonnaise	3 heaping tbs. salad, 2 large leaves lettuce	140
Coleslaw	⅔ cup	70
Carrot and raisin	3 heaping tbs., 2 large leaves lettuce	155
Crab with celery	leaves lettuce 3 heaping tbs., 2 large	140
Fruit, mixed, canned	3 heaping tbs., 2 large leaves lettuce	155
Gelatine with fruit	1 square, 2 large leaves lettuce	140
Gelatine with chopped vegetables	1 square or mold, 2 large leaves lettuce	115
Lettuce with French dressing	8 small leaves, 1 tbs. dressing	80
Lettuce with Russian dressing	8 small leaves, 1 tbs. dressing	60
Lettuce, tomato, mayonnaise	4 leaves lettuce, 1 large tomato, 1 tsp. mayonnaise	80

SOUPS

FOOD	APPROXIMATE AMOUNT	CALORIES
Beef, canned	1 serving, ⅓ can (3½ oz.)	95
Beef with noodles, canned	1 serving, ⅓ can	50
Beef with vegetables	1 serving, ⅓ can	60
Bouillon, canned	1 serving, ⅓ can	30
Bouillon cube, meat extract	1 cube	2
Bouillon cube, vegetable extract	1 cube	8
Chicken Gumbo, canned	1 serving, ⅓ can	50
Chicken with noodles, canned	1 serving, ⅓ can	60
Chicken with rice, canned	1 serving, ⅓ can	35
Clam chowder, canned	1 serving, ⅓ can	65
Consommé, canned	1 serving, ⅓ can	30
Gumbo Creole, canned	1 serving, ⅓ can	65
Vegetable, canned	1 serving, ⅓ can	70
Vegetarian Vegetable, canned	1 serving, ⅓ can	65

VEGETABLES

Asparagus, fresh, cooked	⅔ cup, cut pieces	20
Asparagus, canned, or frozen	6 stalks	20
Beans, green snap, fresh or canned	1 cup, 1" pieces (drained if canned)	30
Beans, green snap, frozen	3½ oz.	35

VEGETABLES (cont.)

FOOD	APPROXIMATE AMOUNT	CALORIES
Beet greens	½ cup	25
Beets, red, canned or fresh	½ cup, diced or sliced (drained if canned)	35
Broccoli, fresh	1 large stalk or ⅔ cup	30
Broccoli, frozen	3½ oz.	25
Brussels sprouts, fresh	½ cup, 5 sprouts	35
Brussels sprouts, frozen	3½ oz.	45
Cabbage, raw, shredded	½ cup	10
Cabbage, cooked	½ cup	20
Carrots, raw	1 large, 2 small, or 1 cup shredded	40
Carrots, cooked	½ cup, diced	25
Cauliflower, raw	1 cup flower pieces	25
Cauliflower, cooked	½ cup	15
Cauliflower, frozen	3½ oz.	25
Celery, raw	3 small inner stalks, 5″ long	10
Celery, cooked	½ cup, diced	10
Chicory or endive	10 small inner leaves	5
Cucumber, raw	½ medium, 7 slices, pared	5
Escarole, raw	9 small inner leaves	5
Kale, fresh, raw, or cooked	½ cup	20
Lettuce, raw	2 large or 5 small leaves	10
Lettuce, romaine, raw	1 large or 2 small leaves	2
Mushrooms, canned solids	½ cup	15

VEGETABLES (cont.)

FOOD	APPROXIMATE AMOUNT	CALORIES
Onions, raw, chopped	1 tablespoon	5
Onions cooked	½ cup, 3 small	40
Parsley, raw	10 small sprigs	5
Pepper, green, raw, or baked	1 shell, empty	20
Pickles		
dill	1 large	10
fresh bread-and-butter	4 slices, 1½" by ¼"	20
sour or mixed	1 large, 4" by 1¾"	25
sweet or mixed	1 pickle, 2" by ⅝"	10
sweet or mixed (chopped)	1 tbs.	15
Potatoes		
baked	1 medium, 2½" diam.	100
boiled	1 medium, 2½" diam.	85
Radishes	2 medium	5
Rice, white, cooked	½ cup	100
Rutabagas, cooked	½ cup	25
Sauerkraut, canned, drained	⅔ cup	20
Spinach, cooked	½ cup, canned; or 3½ oz., frozen	20
Squash, summer, cooked	½ cup scant, diced, fresh; or 3½ oz. frozen	15
Squash, winter, boiled	½ cup scant, mashed	40
Tomatoes, fresh	1 large or 2 small	40
Tomatoes, canned	½ cup	20
Turnip greens, cooked	½ cup	30
Water chestnuts	5	20
Watercress	10 average sprigs	2

MISCELLANEOUS

FOOD	APPROXIMATE AMOUNT	CALORIES
Catsup, tomato	1 tbs.	20
Chili sauce	1 tbs.	20
Garlic bulbs (peeled)	1 bulb	2
Mustard, prepared, brown	1 tsp. level	5
Soy sauce	1 tbs.	10
Vinegar	2 tbs.	5
Worcestershire sauce	1 tsp.	5

DESSERTS

Cake, pound, plain	1 slice, 3″ by 2¾″ by ⅝″	130
Candy		
butterscotch	1 average piece	20
candied cherries	1 large or 2 small	
candied ginger root	1 average piece	15
plain fudge	1 oz.	115
plain milk chocolate	1 oz.	150
Cookies		
ginger snaps	1 small	15
chocolate snaps	1 medium	20
sugar wafers	1 small	15
vanilla wafers	1 small, thin	20
Fig bars, commercial	1 small	55
Fruits (see fruit section)		
Gelatine, lemon	1 serving, ⅔ cup	110
Ice, raspberry, water	½ cup	120
Jello, plain	1 serving, ⅙ pkg.	65

DESSERTS (cont.)

FOOD	APPROXIMATE AMOUNT	CALORIES
Junket	1 serving with ½ cup milk	105
Shortbread, plain	1 piece, 1¾″ square	40
Puddings		
lemon sponge or snow, plain	1 serving	115
Tapioca, minute, plain	½ cup	135

Caloric Content
of Alcoholic Beverages

BEERS AND WINES

BEVERAGE	TOTAL CAL. PER OZ.	TYPICAL SERVING, IN OZ.	TOTAL CAL. PER SERVING
Beer, avg.	15.2	8.0	122
lager	13.5	8.0	108
		12.0	162
malt liquor	15.4	8.0	123
		12.0	185
ale	13.7	8.0	110
		12.0	165
stout	17.6	8.0	141
		12.0	211
Cider	12.1	8.0	96
Wine, table, avg.	24.4	4.0	98
red	23.8	4.0	95
rosé	23.5	4.0	94
dry white	22.6	4.0	90
sweet white	27.4	4.0	110
champagne	24.8	4.0	99
kosher wine	32.8	4.0	131

Wine, fortified, avg.	45.4	2.0	91
dry sherry	39.0	2.0	78
sweet sherry	45.8	2.0	92
port	48.4	2.0	97
muscatel	49.0	2.0	98
vermouth, avg.	39.6	3.0	119
French	34.0	3.0	102
Italian	45.1	3.0	135

DISTILLED SPIRITS (WHISKEY, BRANDY, GIN, VODKA, RUM) *

ALCOHOL PROOF	TOTAL CAL. PER OZ.	TYPICAL SERVING, IN OZ.	TOTAL CAL. PER SERVING
151	125.8	1.5	189
110	91.6	1.5	137
100	83.4	1.5	125
90	75.0	1.5	112
86	71.6	1.5	107
80	66.6	1.5	100

COCKTAILS

COCKTAIL	TOTAL CAL. PER SERVING
Alexander	236
Bloody Mary	217
Bronx	119
Cuba libre	211
Daiquiri	167
Eggnog	219
Gimlet	148

* The caloric content of distilled spirits may be calculated entirely on the basis of alcohol content. For most of them, the yield of total solids is less than 2 calories per serving.

Gin fizz	221
Grasshopper	272
Manhattan (dry)	126
Martini (2:1)	119
Martini (8:1)	143
Marguerita	146
Mint julep	200
Old Fashioned	155
Planter's punch	216
Rum Collins	207
Screwdriver	227
Sherry flip	187
Sidecar	182
Stinger	181
Tom and Jerry	218
Tom Collins	217
Whiskey Sour	163
Zombie	549

* The caloric values of these cocktails are based on what are believed to be widely used recipes and may vary according to special formulas employed. In most examples, the total quantity includes about 2 oz. of distilled spirits. For these calculations, it is assumed that the distilled spirits are used at alcohol concentrations most frequently dispensed in the United States: 86-proof whiskey, gin and vodka; 80-proof brandy and most rums.

Carbohydrate, Protein, and Fat Content of Foods

Showing amounts of carbohydrate (C), protein (P), and fat (F) present in 100-gm. (3½-ounce) portions of common foods. 1 gram C or P = 4 calories; 1 gram F = 9 calories.

CEREALS, BREAD, AND OTHER FLOUR PRODUCTS

FOOD	100-GRAM PORTION (HOUSEHOLD MEASUREMENT)	C	P	F
Bread, white, rye, or whole wheat	3½ slices, ½″ thick	50	9	3
Cake or cookies, without fruit or icing	1 slice (3″ by 3″ by 1½″)	65	6	9
Cereal, whole wheat, rice, rye, or oat, dry	⅓ cup	19	4	2
Crackers, graham	10 to 12 large	72	9	9
Crackers, matzo	6″ diam.	17	2	0
Crackers, soda	25 (2″ by 2″)	73	10	9

CEREALS, BREAD, AND OTHER FLOUR PRODUCTS (cont.)

FOOD	100-GRAM PORTION (HOUSEHOLD MEASUREMENT)	C	P	F
Doughnuts	2	52	7	22
Hominy, cooked	½ cup	15	2	0
Macaroni, cooked	⅔ cup	18	3	0
Macaroni, raw	¾ cup	74	13	1
Noodles, cooked	½ cup	20	4	0
Rice, white, polished, dry	½ cup	76	7	0
Spaghetti, cooked	½ cup	20	4	0

DAIRY PRODUCTS

FOOD	100-GRAM PORTION	C	P	F
Milk, whole	⅖ cup	5	4	4
Milk, skim	⅖ cup	5	4	0
Milk, evaporated	⅖ cup	10	7	8
Milk, powdered, skim	¾ cup	52	36	1
Milk, malted, dry	¾ cup	72	15	9
Buttermilk	½ cup	5	4	1
Cream, 10% (light)	⅖ cup	5	4	12
Cream 20% (average)	⅖ cup	5	3	19
Cream, 40% (heavy)	⅖ cup	3	2	41
Ice cream (without fruit or nuts)	½ cup	20	4	13
Butter (or margarine)	10 squares (1″ by 1″ by ½″)	0	1	81

DAIRY PRODUCTS (cont.)

FOOD	100-GRAM PORTION (HOUSEHOLD MEASUREMENT)	C	P	F
Cheese, American	1 slice	2	27	32
Cheese, cottage	6 level tbs.	4	20	1
Cheese, cream	5 squares (1″ by 1″ by ¾″)	2	7	34
Cheese, other	⅖ cup	2	20	32

EGGS

Egg, whole	1 medium (60 gm.)	0	6	6
Egg white	1 white only	0	3	0
Egg yolk	1 yolk only	0	3	6

FISH (raw, unless otherwise specified)

Bass	2 slices (4″ by 2″ by ½″)	0	20	2
Clams, meat only	½ cup	5	11	1
Cod	2 slices (4″ by 2″ by ½″)	0	20	1
Crabmeat, canned	⅔ cup	1	17	3
Fish, other	⅔ cup	0	19	8
Halibut	2 slices (4″ by 2″ by ½″)	0	18	6
Herring	½ medium fish	0	20	7

FISH (raw, unless otherwise specified) (cont.)

FOOD	100-GRAM PORTION (HOUSEHOLD MEASUREMENT)	C	P	F
Herring, smoked	½ medium fish	0	37	16
Lobster, fresh or canned	¾ cup meat	0	18	1
Oysters, meat only	4 or 5 large	5	8	1
Salmon, fresh or canned	¾ cup	0	21	12
Sardines, canned	4 large or 10 small	0	23	20
Scallops	½ cup	3	15	0
Shrimp	½ cup	1	18	1

FRUITS—GROUP A (approximately 5% C)

Avocado	½ of 4"-long fruit	3	2	26
Muskmelon (cantaloupe or honeydew)	¼ melon of 5" diam.	5	1	0
Watermelon, edible fruit portion	1 slice (2" by 2" by 2")	6	0	0

FRUITS—GROUP B (approximately 10% C)

Blackberries	½ cup	8	11	1
Cranberries, cooked	¼ cup	10	1	1
Currants	½ cup	10	2	0
Gooseberries	⅔ cup	8	1	0
Grapefruit	½ of 4" diam. or ⅝ cup juice	10	0	0

FRUITS—GROUP B (approximately 10% C) (cont.)

FOOD	100-GRAM PORTION (HOUSEHOLD MEASUREMENT)	PROPORTIONS (IN GRAMS)		
		C	P	F
Lemon	1 2½"-long fruit or ½ cup juice	8	1	0
Papaya	¼ of 5" diam.	9	1	0
Tangerine	2 small fruit or ½ cup juice	9	1	0

FRUITS—GROUP C (approximately 15% C)

Apple	1 small or ¾ medium	14	0	0
Apple juice	½ cup	13	0	0
Applesauce	½ cup	13	0	0
Apricots, fresh	1½ average	13	1	0
Blueberries	⅔ cup fruit or ⅔ cup juice	15	1	1
Grapes	½ cup	15	1	1
Huckleberries	⅔ cup fruit or ⅖ cup juice	14	0	0
Lime	1 2½"-long fruit	13	0	0
Loganberries	⅔ cup	14	1	1
Mulberries	⅔ cup	13	0	0
Nectarines	2 medium	14	0	0
Orange	1 medium fruit or ⅖ cup juice	13	0	0
Peach	1 medium, 2½" diam.	12	1	0

FRUITS—GROUP C (approximately 15% C) (cont.)

FOOD	100-GRAM PORTION (HOUSEHOLD MEASUREMENT)	C	P	F
Pear	1 medium	14	1	0
Pineapple, fresh or canned	⅔ cup or 1 slice 3″ thick	14	0	0
Pineapple juice	½ cup	14	0	0
Plums, fresh	3 of 1½″ diam. each	12	1	0
Quince, fresh	⅓ medium quince	12	0	0
Raspberries	⅔ cup fruit or ½ cup juice	12	1	1

FRUITS—GROUP D (approximately 20% C)

FOOD	100-GRAM PORTION (HOUSEHOLD MEASUREMENT)	C	P	F
Banana	1 medium or ½ large	22	1	0
Cherries	⅔ cup	17	1	1
Figs, fresh	2 medium, 1½″ diam.	18	1	0
Grape juice	½ cup	19	0	0
Persimmon, Japanese	1 large	18	1	0
Prune juice, canned	½ glass	18	0	0
Prunes, fresh	3 to 4	19	1	0

FRUITS—GROUP E (above 20% C)

FOOD	100-GRAM PORTION (HOUSEHOLD MEASUREMENT)	PROPORTIONS (IN GRAMS)		
		C	P	F
Cherries, maraschino	½ cup	50	0	0
Currants, dried	½ cup	70	2	0
Dates, fresh	18 medium	65	2	0
Dates, dried	14 medium	78	2	3
Figs, dried	8 to 10	68	4	0
Persimmons, native, fresh	2 small	28	1	0
Prunes, dried	10 medium	65	2	0
Raisins, dried	⅔ cup	75	3	3

MEAT AND POULTRY (raw, unless otherwise specified)

FOOD	MEASUREMENT	C	P	F
Bacon	10 slices (2″ by 4″ by ⅛″)	0	9	65
Bacon, crisp-cooked	20 slices (2″ by 3″ by ⅛″)	0	30	50
Beef, medium fat, medium roasted	2 slices (2″ by 3″ by 1″)	0	20	11
Beef, lean, broiled	2 slices (2″ by 3″ by 1″)	0	28	5
Beef, fatty, medium roasted	2 slices (2″ by 3″ by 1″)	0	13	18
Chicken or duck	2 slices	0	21	5
Frankfurter, all meat	2 average	1	19	18
Ham, fresh, lean	2 slices (2″ by 2″ by ½″)	0	25	14

MEAT AND POULTRY (raw, unless otherwise specified) (cont.)

FOOD	100-GRAM PORTION (HOUSEHOLD MEASUREMENT)	C	P	F
Ham, fresh, fatty	2 slices (4″ by 3″ by ½″)	0	12	40
Heart, beef	2 slices (2″ by 3″ by ½″)	0	16	20
Heart, pork	1 slice (2″ by 3″ by 1″)	0	17	6
Kidney	½ cup	0	16	6
Lamb (or mutton)	2 pieces (1″ by 4″ by 1″)	0	19	15
Lamb (or mutton) chops	2	0	20	22
Liver	2 slices (3″ by 2″ by ½″)	0	20	5
Pork, lean	1 piece (2″ by 3″ by 3″)	0	16	24
Sausage, all meat	6 (3″ by ¾″)	0	18	38
Tongue	5 slices, ¼″ thick	0	16	15
Turkey	2 slices (4″ by 3″ by ½″)	0	22	18
Veal, medium fat	2 slices (2″ by 3″ by ½″)	0	20	8

VEGETABLES—GROUP A (approximately 5% C)

FOOD	100-GRAM PORTION	C	P	F
Artichokes, French	1 medium	3	1	0
Asparagus	½ cup tips or 10 stalks	3	1	0

VEGETABLES—GROUP A (approximately 5% C) (cont.)

FOOD	100-GRAM PORTION (HOUSEHOLD MEASUREMENT)	C	P	F
Beans, green	¾ cup	3	1	0
Beet greens	½ cup	4	2	0
Broccoli	⅔ cup	4	3	0
Brussels sprouts	10 sprouts	4	1	0
Cabbage	⅔ to 1 cup	4	1	0
Cauliflower	⅔ cup	2	1	0
Celery	2 hearts or 4 stalks	3	1	0
Chard leaves	2 to 3 cups	4	3	0
Cucumber	½ cup	2	1	0
Eggplant	¾ cup	4	1	0
Endive	2 small	2	1	0
Escarole	⅔ small head	2	1	0
Kale	⅔ cup	5	2	0
Leek	¾ cup	5	2	0
Lettuce	⅓ small head	2	1	0
Mushrooms	½ cup	1	1	0
Okra	½ cup	4	1	0
Pepper, green	1 medium, 3″ to 4″ long	4	1	0
Pumpkin	½ cup	6	1	0
Radishes	10 medium	3	1	0
Rhubarb	⅔ cup	3	1	0

VEGETABLES—GROUP A (approximately 5% C) (cont.)

FOOD	100-GRAM PORTION (HOUSEHOLD MEASUREMENT)	C	P	F
Sauerkraut	⅔ cup	3	1	0
Spinach	½ cup	2	1	0
Squash, summer	⅔ cup	3	1	0
Tomatoes	1 medium or ½ cup	4	1	0
Turnip, beet or greens	½ cup	5	1	0
Watercress	1 medium bunch	2	1	0

VEGETABLES—GROUP B (approximately 10% C)

FOOD	100-GRAM PORTION	C	P	F
Beans, dry soy	½ cup	7	35	18
Beet root	½ cup	9	2	0
Carrots	⅔ cup	8	1	0
Dandelion greens	½ cup cooked	7	3	1
Onion, white	½ cup (5 or 6 small)	9	2	0
Peas, green (fresh or canned)	½ cup	9	4	0
Pepper, red	1 medium, 3″ to 4″ long	7	1	1
Rutabaga	⅔ cup	7	1	0
Squash, winter	¾ cup	7	1	0

VEGETABLES—GROUP C (approximately 15% C)

FOOD	100-GRAM PORTION (HOUSEHOLD MEASUREMENT)	PROPORTIONS (IN GRAMS) C	P	F
Beans, lima	½ cup	15	4	0
Parsnips	½ cup	16	2	1

VEGETABLES—GROUP D (approximately 20% C)

Beans, baked, canned	½ cup	19	6	2
Beans, dry	½ cup	62	22	2
Beans, kidney, canned	½ cup	17	7	0
Chili sauce	⅓ cup	20	0	0
Corn	⅓ cup	19	3	1
Lentils	½ cup	57	25	1
Potato, white	1 medium, 2½" diam.	19	2	1
Potato chips	4 cups	49	7	37
Potato, sweet	1 small or ½ medium	26	3	0
Succotash, canned	⅔ cup	18	4	1

MISCELLANEOUS FOODS

Beer	⅖ glass	4	0	0
Broth, clear	½ cup	0	0	0
Carbonated drinks	⅖ glass	8 to 16	0	0
Catsup, tomato	⅖ cup	24	2	0

MISCELLANEOUS FOODS (cont.)

FOOD	100-GRAM PORTION (HOUSEHOLD MEASUREMENT)	PROPORTIONS (IN GRAMS) C	P	F
Chocolate, sweet, dry	⅖ cup	60	2	25
Chocolate, unsweetened, dry	⅖ cup	25	12	52
Cocoa, dry, unsweetened	¾ cup	38	18	20
Coconut, prepared	1 cup	52	4	39
Cod liver oil	⅖ cup	0	0	0
Custard	½ cup	5	6	7
Dextrose	⅖ cup	100	0	0
Fat, cooking	⅖ cup	0	0	100
Flour	1½ cups	76	11	1
Gelatine, dry	⅔ cup	0	85	0
Honey	⅓ cup	81	0	0
Jelly	⅓ cup	70	0	0
Lard (or other shortening)	⅖ cup	0	0	100
Marmalade	⅓ cup	65	1	0
Mayonnaise	⅖ cup	0	2	75
Molasses	½ cup	60	0	0
Nuts, miscellaneous (meats)	3½ oz.	20	2	60
Oils, salad and cooking	⅖ cup	0	0	100
Olives, ripe or green	18	3	2	15
Pickles, sour	⅓ cup	2	0.5	0
Pickles, sweet, mixed	1 cup	25	1	0

MISCELLANEOUS FOODS (cont.)

FOOD	100-GRAM PORTION (HOUSEHOLD MEASUREMENT)	PROPORTIONS (IN GRAMS) C	P	F
Popcorn, popped	6 cups	80	12	5
Salad dressing	⅓ cup	15	5	10
Soup, commercial, undiluted (see labels)	⅖ cup	10	3	2
Soup, creamed	½ cup	4	2	13
Soybean, dry	½ cup	12	34	18
Soybean, fresh	⅔ cup	6	13	7
Starch, corn	¾ cup	87	1	0
Sugar, granulated	⅖ cup	100	0	0
Tapioca pudding	⅔ cup	28	3	3
Vinegar	⅖ cup	4	0	0
Yeast	100 gm.	8	8	0

Average Carbohydrate Content of Alcoholic Beverages

BEVERAGE	TYPICAL SERVING, IN OZ.	GMS. CARBOHYDRATE PER SERVING
Beer, lager	8.0	12.0
	12.0	18.0
Wine, table		
red	4.0	0.3
rosé	4.0	1.3
dry white	4.0	0.4
sweet white	4.0	4.9
champagne	4.0	1.8
Wine, fortified		
muscatel	2.0	7.0
port	2.0	7.0
dry sherry	2.0	1.2
medium sherry	2.0	1.9
sweet sherry	2.0	6.4
vermouth, French	3.0	4.2
vermouth, Italian	3.0	13.9
Distilled spirits	1.5	trace

Measurement Conversion Table

EQUIVALENTS BY WEIGHT

1 pound (16 ounces)	=	453.6 grams
1 ounce	=	28.35 grams
3½ ounces	=	100.00 grams

EQUIVALENTS BY VOLUME
(all measurements level)

1 quart	=	4 cups
1 cup	=	8 fluid ounces
	=	½ pint
	=	16 tablespoons
2 tablespoons	=	1 fluid ounce
1 tablespoon	=	3 teaspoons
1 pound of butter or margarine	=	4 sticks—2 cups
1 stick butter or margarine	=	½ cup or 16 pats

The cup measure refers to the standard measuring cup of 8 fluid ounces or ½ liquid pint. The ounce refers to 1/16 of a pound avoirdupois, unless fluid ounces is indicated. The weight of a fluid ounce varies according to the food measured.

INDEX

Index

low-calorie 84
low-fat 113
processed 31, 80, 81
rich 78
spicy 107
Food-tasting 42
Forty (age) 44
Frankfurters 95
Fruits
citrus 84
canned 98
dried 95
frozen 98
pickled 102
spiced 102
Fruit for dieters 78, 117
Fruit as natural carbohydrate 31
Fruit for heart patients 113
Fruit low in protein, calories 82

Gallbladder ailments 106-107
Gallstones 71-72
Game 81
Garlic 102
Gastrointestinal disorders 74
Gingerbread 101
Glycerine 31
Glycosuria 68-69
Golf 35
Grams 32
Grapefruit 102, 105
Gravies 78, 102, 113
Griddle cakes 101
Goose 95
Gout 108-109
Gums, Vegetable 74-75

Ham 109
Hamburgers, Fatty 95
Harvard University 49
Health
anxiety about 14
considered in reducing 28
hazards to 49, 52
Heart, 81, 95
Heart attacks 113-114

Heart disease: *see* Heart trouble
"Heart factor" 63
Heart palpitation 74
Heart patients 35
Heart trouble 13
amphetamines 74
death rate 60
exercise 35, 36
formula diets 76
reducing 28
smoking 49
Heat 31-32
Heats 59
Hemp 48
Herbs 118
Heredity
diabetes 68
"glandular obesity" 17
heart disease 61, 65
menopause 58, 59
overweight 16
Herring 98
Hips 59
Hobbies 36
Holland 27
Honey 95
Horseradish 21
Hours, Regular 44
Hunger 32, 74
Hypertension 61

Ice cream 31, 98, 113
Immigrants 19
Inhalation 36
Insomnia 55
Insulin 67, 69
Insurance companies 60
Interests 36
Iron 32
deficiency 32-33
high deposits in arteries 63
cereals 82
meat 80
milk 82
Irritability 59